THE HIDDEN KNOWLEDGE OF EGYPTIAN MYTHOLOGY

By Mary Gemming, Ph.D.

With illustrations by the author

© 2021 Mary Gemming, Ph.D. All rights reserved.

No part of this book may be reproduced, stored in a retrieval system, or transmitted by any means without the written permission of the author.

AuthorHouse™
1663 Liberty Drive
Bloomington, IN 47403
www.authorhouse.com
Phone: 833-262-8899

Because of the dynamic nature of the Internet, any web addresses or links contained in this book may have changed since publication and may no longer be valid. The views expressed in this work are solely those of the author and do not necessarily reflect the views of the publisher, and the publisher hereby disclaims any responsibility for them.

Any people depicted in stock imagery provided by Getty Images are models, and such images are being used for illustrative purposes only.
Certain stock imagery © Getty Images.

This book is printed on acid-free paper.

ISBN: 978-1-6655-2287-8 (sc)
ISBN: 978-1-6655-2288-5 (e)

Library of Congress Control Number: 2021908172

Print information available on the last page.

Published by AuthorHouse 05/03/2021

authorHOUSE

OTHER BOOKS BY MARY GEMMING:

Discovering Treasures of Peace
Mystical Secrets of the Stars

This book is dedicated to Ahmed Fayed of Cairo, Egypt who was considered one of the most knowledgeable Egyptologists concerning ancient Egypt. He was the Egyptologist for the Association of Research and Enlightenment in Virginia Beach, Virginia. Ahmed is no longer with us, but he will always be remembered for his great generosity and love for humanity.

ACKNOWLEDGMENTS

I wish to thank the Association for Research and Enlightenment (A.R.E.) for the wonderful work that they do. My life has changed tremendously since becoming an A.R.E. member several years ago. The A.R.E. conferences with motivating speakers have left lasting inspirations with me. In this book I have quoted some of the Edgar Cayce Readings referring to Egypt.

Edgar Cayce Readings © 1971, 1993—2007 by the Edgar Cayce Foundation. All rights reserved.

I also wish to thank The Academy For Future Science for their extraordinary work in their publications by J. J. Hurtak, as well as Kim Converse, an AFFS facilitator and accomplished musician for the Keys of Enoch Study Group at the Cosmic Center of Spiritual Light in Sarasota, Florida.

Hurtak, J. J. (1973) *The Book of Knowledge: the Keys of Enoch®,* Los Gatos; The Academy For Future Science.www.keysofenoch.org.

FOREWORD

In this outstanding, insightful manuscript, Mary has taken the ancient symbology and history of Egypt to a very spiritual level.

Mary's in-depth knowledge of astrology brings the reader to a high level of understanding of this accurate information and science, based upon the history and myths of ancient Egypt. Mary's revelations of the connections between astrology and Egypt will leave the reader captivated with its accuracy.

After 32 trips to Egypt, I found this particular book on the myths and history of Egypt one of the best I have ever read.

Read, learn and enjoy some of the most interesting theories on Egypt you will ever experience. This is a book you will recommend to your friends and family.

--John Davis

Author of *Messiah and the Second Coming, Revelation for Our Time,* and *Be the Light of the World.*

John Davis is the Director of Coptic Fellowship International, a modern philosophy based on the Mystery Schools of ancient Egypt. As president of World Light Travels, and Egyptologist, John has conducted tours to Egypt and other sacred sites.

TABLE OF CONTENTS

PREFACE
The fascination of Egyptian culture—its carefully prepared system of knowledge. How ageless wisdom was revealed. The ancient Egyptians have something to tell us.

INTRODUCTION
Each of us is connected to a star. Previous ages were more advanced than currently recognized. Astronomy and Astrology are related to mythology. The religion of ancient Egypt was based on astrology and mythology. The Egyptian system of knowledge drew Greek philosophers to the Nile. Plato was initiated in the Great Pyramid. Symbolism of the god, Hapi, the hippopotamus, and Renenuter, the nourishing snake. The connection between Egypt and Ethiopia. Coptic origins.

CHAPTER ONE
The importance of the eye and what it symbolizes. Anubis and the Eye of Horus. The presence of the Zodiac in ancient religions of Egypt, Jerusalem, India and China. The story of Cheiro. Famous personalities who consult astrologers. Since Astrology is an important aid to help individuals, why did astrology get put down? A surprising answer. How Astrology helps humanity. The mystery of the understanding of Uranus by the ancients. The real meaning behind the worshipping of the Sun. The conflict between the Egyptian priesthood and Akhenaton, and the result of the conflict.

CHAPTER TWO
What we know from History. New evidence of the early civilizations and their use of astrology. The timetable of ancient Egypt. Dynasties, including the early pre-dynastic period, the Old Kingdom, the Middle Kingdom, the Early New Kingdom, the Late New Kingdom, the Late Period,

and the period covering Cleopatra. Edgar Cayce, the "Sleeping Prophet." The Akashic Records and the Essenes. Egypt's control through the religion of the Pharaohs.

CHAPTER THREE

The Pantheon of Gods and what it was. All Egyptian temples were aligned with a star system. The depiction of Rah, the begetter of all gods. The three forms of the Sun god. Ptah, Sekhemet and Nefertum. Khnum and Neith. Amun-Rah, Mut and Khonsu, the Egyptian Trinity. Shu, Tefnut and Geb. Osiris, Hathor and Horus. Bastet, the cat goddess. Various Egyptian myths, including: The Creation Myth, The Osiris Myth, The Myth of the Afterlife and Hell, The Ramses Myth, The Myth of the Imperfect State of the World and the Cosmic Cycle, The Benu Bird Myth, The Egyptian/Greek/Roman Myth of Amun, The Myth of the Sphinx, The Myth of the Lord of the Nile.

CHAPTER FOUR

The mystery of Hathor. The sculptured head figures at the Temple of Hathor and at the Temple of Isis. The Sirius mystery. The secret knowledge of the ancient Dogons. Dogon Tribe Symbols. The Seven Wonders of the World. The Mystery of the Great Pyramid of Giza. Connections between the King's Chamber and Orion, the Queens Chamber and Sirius. The mystery of the Sphinx.

CHAPTER FIVE

The earliest calendar. The adoption of the unique Egyptian calendar. The Egyptian Zodiac and its difference in time periods. The significance of the Egyptian New Year. The two versions of Serapis: Serapis Bey and the blending of Osiris and apis, the bull god.

CHAPTER SIX

The beginning of the Egyptian Zodiac, connecting it with Aries and the god Khnum and his consort, Neith. The Egyptian month of Pharmuthi from March 27 to April 25. Khnum as the shaper of humanity upon the celestial potter's wheel.

CHAPTER SEVEN

Taurus and Ptah. The Egyptian month of Pachons from April 26 to May 25. Ptah as the developer. His wife was the lioness Sekhmet; their son, Nefertum.

CHAPTER EIGHT

Gemini and Horus. The Egyptian month of Paoni from May 26 to June 24. This is the period representing Horus, the god of the Sky and Protector of the Pharaohs.

CHAPTER NINE

Cancer and Nephthys. The Egyptian month of Epep from June 25 to July 24. Nephthys, sister of Isis, joined Isis in caring for Osiris after he was killed.

CHAPTER TEN

Leo and Sekhmet. The Egyptian month of Mesore from July 25 to August 28. Sekhmet, "the powerful one," and Tefnut and Bastet.

CHAPTER ELEVEN

Virgo and Isis. The Egyptian month of Thoth from August 29 to September 28. Isis as the archetype of the divine mother, savior and healer.

CHAPTER TWELVE

Libra and Anubis. The Egyptian month of Paopi from September 29 to October 27. The half-dog, half-man Anubis as supervisor of the journey to the afterlife and adornment of burial artifacts. He is also the tester of hearts and balance.

CHAPTER THIRTEEN

Scorpio and Set, the lord of the barren desert. The Egyptian month of Athor from October 28 to November 26. The evil god, Set, and how he enticed Osiris. The price Set paid for killing

Osiris. The scorpion goddess, Selkit, who guarded the pharaoh's sarcophagus. Selkit's connection to the Mayans.

CHAPTER FOURTEEN
Sagittarius and Thoth. The Egyptian month of Cheoak from November 27 to December 26. Thoth, the ibis-headed scribe of the gods recorded the deeds of a person's life on earth and guided the deceased.

CHAPTER FIFTEEN
Capricorn and Hathor. The Egyptian month of Toobi from December 27 to January 25. Hathor, the wife of Horus, had the honor of being called the mother queen of all gods and goddesses. Her temples were devoted to healing, joy, love and entertainment. The real meaning of the Hathors.

CHAPTER SIXTEEN
Aquarius and Amon-Rah. The Egyptian month of Mechir from January 26 to February 24. The reign of Amun-Rah, Lord of the Heaven, and Light of the World. His temple at Karnak took over 2,000 years to build, encompassing 247 acres, the largest religious site on the planet. The Divine Trio of Thebes.

CHAPTER SEVENTEEN
Pisces and Osiris. The Egyptian month of Phamenoth from February 25 to March 26. The reign of Osiris, god of the spirit world. How Isis revived and saved Osiris. The important constellation that was Osiris's connection to the heavens.

CHAPTER EIGHTEEN
Revelations through the Hermetic Texts. The mysterious chambers above the King's Chamber. The mystical Duat. Egypt as an image of heaven.

CHAPTER NINETEEN
Thoth-Hermes Trismegistus. The Embodiment of the Universal Mind.

CHAPTER TWENTY
The Mysterious Temple at Dendera. The oldest known of all Zodiacs. What happened to the original representation of the Great Zodiac. Artifacts found from the Old Kingdom and Middle Kingdom. The annual festival and procession between Edfu and Dendera, through the Hall of Appearances, the Hall of Offerings, to the Holy of the Holies, to the roof chapel climaxing with the unity of Hathor with the sun disc. The magical healing center where miraculous cures took place. The god Bes and the goddess Tauret. Question of the prominence of Cancer in the Dendera Zodiac.

CONCLUSION
The choice of polarities determines a positive or negative outcome. Seeking an experience of being alive. The land of Egypt has its own song. Egypt as the mother of civilization. The Sacred Sermon that tells of sages who lived before the Great Flood. The mystery of the airplane type of symbols at the Temple of Osiris at Abydos.

APPENDIX : Astrological Symbols.

PREFACE

Perhaps it began when the Greek historian, Herodotus, wrote about Egypt in 500 B.C. However, there is no question that humanity has been fascinated with its ancient culture that reportedly lasted more than 3,000 years. And even though we were fascinated by Egypt, how much did we really know about this mysterious culture? It reminds me of a comical answer that a sixth grade student gave on a history test about Egypt: "Ancient Egypt was inhabited by mummies and they all wrote in hydraulics."

Then the discovery of the treasures of the young pharaoh, Tutankhamen, by Howard Carter in the Valley of the Kings in 1923 unlocked an exquisite artistry never before seen in the modern world. The artistic drawings in this and other tombs revealed evidence through unique symbols that Egypt at one time was the center of the most erudite Mystery Schools ever to grace this planet.

Long ago, the Egyptian sages taught a doctrine of metaphysics that appealed to the higher inspiration of minds. This carefully prepared system of knowledge attracted such thinkers as Pythagoras and Plato, who embarked on the journey from Greece to Heliopolis, Egypt, to seek admission into the great initiations of the Mystery School Center, as you will see.

The ancients established that man is never truly wise until he can understand the riddle of his existence, and the temples of initiation were the only depositories of that special knowledge which would enable him to unravel the Gordian knot of his human nature. The Gordian knot refers to Gordius, the ancient king of Phrygia, who tied a knot which was to be undone by only the one who could rule Asia, and this was eventually done by Alexander the Great. The Gordian knot has been used to pertain to the ability to get out of a difficulty, instantaneously.

The ageless truths of life were revealed through secret societies, whose members were the leading scholars of the time. These hidden truths included the knowledge of a secret universe beyond the material, visible realm. Although this reality had been secluded from the masses, it had been passed down from generation to generation through the ancient mystery schools. One of the purposes of these schools was to safeguard the sacred teachings from ill-intentioned individuals who might have perverted the teachings for selfish reasons. Actually, the ancient truths were exposed to view at all times, but not recognized because of their concealment in symbols. As soon as humanity learns to read the language of symbolism, the hidden veil will fall from the eyes of the human race. They shall realize that the truth has always been in the world, but unrecognized except for those indoctrinated by the Ascended Masters who reveal only to the disciples who have pledged to serve the world.

The initiation practices of ancient Egypt have been preserved in such traditions as the Coptic religion, Freemasonry, the Rosicrucians, Ascended Master Teachings, and in other avenues which are generally unknown to the masses. Although the Knights Templar retained most of the Eastern mysteries, they were destroyed by the Inquisition, which was able to confiscate the great wealth that the Knights Templar had acquired. Fortunately, some of them survived, but had to go underground for protection. The political reasons behind the murders of the Templars are a long story in itself.

By the early 1300's, esoteric disciples learned to be cautious about using the terminology of alchemists, astrologers, Masons and Rosicrucians. By then, much fear had been created in the masses of anything pertaining to secret teachings-- which were labeled "occult," or the workings of the devil. And so the legends of King Arthur, Hercules and Robin Hood became a pattern of heroes, in order to carry on the plan for enlightenment for the planet through the actions of a brotherhood, known as the Brotherhood of Light with spiritual retreats around the world. In correspondence to the Brotherhood of the Himalayas, and the Egyptian Thoth, who helped to perfect humanity through art and illumination, the writers of inspiration sought to perfect human nature through the liberal arts.

The ancient astrologers and alchemists performed an amazing task. They provided a bridge between ancient magic and science. It is known that Tibet had its ancient magic, as did Egypt. The transmutation of metals into a finer substance, such as gold (known as alchemy), was not uncommon, and eventually this evolved into the transmutation of the physical body into a divine body. The sacred knowledge of Egypt's most brilliant time in the past has been preserved for those who are willing to seek the higher path of life.

The Egyptian gods no longer have the power they once possessed. However, they are frozen in time in the ancient temples and myths, where their memory lingers on. And for the Egyptians, this was the fulfillment of an important goal: never to be forgotten. I venture to say that this was for a good reason. It is because the ancient Egyptians had something to tell us, something that was important for the human race.

This question has been frequently asked: What are we looking for? Consciously, or unconsciously, we are looking for a way to find transcendence in this world of experience. We need a real sense of awareness, a belonging to something higher than what we see in everyday life. Spiritual teachers call it "Self-realization." The soul is always seeking a transcendent experience where it can surpass the material self into a higher quality of life that is everlasting.

Sometimes we settle for less, losing hope that we can reach what we were truly meant for …something higher than a mere existence in the physical things of life. Some individuals are not yet aware of their soul purpose in life. When one is aware of his/her destiny, it brings a motivation that empowers all faculties, aided by the universe, to fulfill something that no one else can fulfill but that one individual. Then again, the drive to fulfill a soul destiny is not always known consciously, but subconsciously. That is why it is beneficial to know oneself and to pursue the ancient mysteries of soul enfoldment. The carrying out of the soul purpose leads the way to the All That There Is.

INTRODUCTION

"Astrology is a science in itself and contains an illumination body of knowledge. It taught me many things. And I am greatly indebted to it.

"Geophysical evidence reveals the power of the stars and the planets in relation to the terrestrial.

"In turn, Astrology reinforces this power to some extent. This is why Astrology is like a life-giving elixir for mankind."

--Albert Einstein

The stars in all the heavens are but a reflection of the greater universe of God from where you came. The ancient Egyptians believed that each of us is connected to a star. In other words, the physical self is connected to a spiritual self in a higher realm, as revealed by the Egyptian myth of Osiris and Horus. Interestingly enough, even the Dogon tribe of West Africa had a similar symbology.

When we talk about stars, we are talking about astronomy and astrology. "Astro" is Greek for *star* and "nomy" is Greek for *law*. Therefore, astronomy is the law of the stars. And astrology means the lore of the stars, since "ology" means "reason, lore or myth." Moreover, astrology encompasses the study of planets and principles that govern the universe. At one time, astronomy and astrology went hand in hand for many years, and were one science. Astrology was the sister science of astronomy until the 17th Century. Even the *Enclyclopedia Brittanica* defines astrology as a science: "The ancient art or science of divining the fate and future of human beings from indications given by the position of the stars and other heavenly bodies."

In the Bible, the Book of Revelation is an initiation text with its roots in the ancient star culture of the first century A. D. The Bible is encoded with the mystic symbols and myths of the stars, a reflection of the codes of ancient traditions. To cite just one example, in Luke, Chapter 21, verse 25:

"And there will be signs in sun and moon and stars, and upon the earth distress of nations in perplexity at the roaring of the sea and the waves."

The continuous appearance of Ageless Wisdom, that inner, mystical teaching handed down from remote times, has always attracted the attention of seeking minds. It has been compared to a Golden Thread, much like a spiritual truth that connects through humanity from century to century. The truth is always present, but it depends on the state of consciousness of humanity to be able to see it. And life has a way of trying to get our attention, sometimes through an avatar such as Buddha or Jesus, or with a New Age movement, of which there have been many throughout time. It is difficult for some individuals to realize that previous ages have risen and fallen, and that some were more advanced and more in touch with the Ageless Wisdom than ours.

When we stop to think about it, astronomy/astrology has much to do with mythology, because the planets and constellations are named after gods and goddesses or mythological beings. Mythology is a secret opening for the marvelous creative energies of the cosmos, enabling it to pour through its powers into the activities of humanity on the earth plane. The magic of myths and legends handed down from generation to generation somehow cannot die, but lives on in a mysterious way. The magic lives on as if it has a life of its own, and will not be quenched by anyone or anything. The magic of lore lies throughout all of the cultures of the earth, whichever you can think of –Egyptian, Hebrew, Tibetan, Hindu, etc. And while we are speaking of these cultures, I want to mention that J. J. Hurtak in *The Book of Knowledge: The Keys of Enoch,* says that the ancient tongues of Egyptian, Hebrew, Tibetan, Sanskrit and Chinese were used in a spiritual way to connect to the Masters of Wisdom through the sound vibration that they produce.

Now, let me pose this question: Does all of this relate to the Occult Law which said that spiritual truths could only be taught in codes or myths, until recent times when the overall consciousness of humanity rose over 50 %, allowing for higher teachings? Or is it relative because this is how people can relate best, by symbolic teachings? The answer is yes for both parts.

We have inherited myths and legends that were created to teach truths that had been encoded in symbols. And symbols are an international universal language.

What do we mean by mythology? Myth means lore or legend, and then mythology is the study of legends. The religion of ancient Egypt was based on Mythology and Astrology. Mythology is the fire, the energy, which has driven societies. Mythology connects each generation to the generations who follow. Each culture relies on these essential stories, which serve to preserve the heritage of the past, as well as to assure the progression of the species.

In the book, *The Dreams of Reason*, Rene Dubos said that society, no matter how primitive, is always arranged around myths and customs that go beyond the necessities of life.

Here is something to think about. In the book, *Law of Life*, A.D. K. Luk wrote that many names that were used in mythology are the names of real, Great Beings who were known in the ancient past. The fall of man created a great density that hid the higher reality of life. The memory of these Great Beings, who once lived in Lemuria, remained only in myth, except for the teachings of the Masters of Wisdom. I will touch more on this later.

The Egyptian Hierophants taught a system of knowledge that drew to the Nile delta such Greek philosophers as Pythagoras and Plato, who deemed it important to personally verify the ancient wisdom of the Egyptians. In fact, every religion possessed a system of higher truths that were preserved for those who were dedicated to serving humanity and were able to advance in consciousness. Pythagorus must have qualified because he spent twenty-two years studying in Egypt.

I was fascinated to learn that Plato (428 to 347 B. C.) had been initiated into the "Greater Mysteries" at age 49 in a subterranean hall of the Great Pyramid. Manly Hall states in *The Secret Teachings of All Ages* that after three months of Initiation in the Great Pyramid of Giza, Plato was given a mission to do the work of the Great Order, just as had been given to the Greek initiates preceding him, Pythagoras, and Orpheus.

Plato wrote *Timaeus,* a work that influenced astrological theories. He showed that myths represented the earlier form of scientific expression, rather than being just legends. Plato described the universe as a living entity, composed of four elements (air, water, earth, fire) each possessing a different molecular form. Yet he explained that the four elements were harmoniously interconnected.

Plato also wrote about astrology when the twelve signs were still ruled by gods and goddesses. Further, astrology was linked to myths from Babylon and Assyria, as well as Egypt. The myths that are connected to the signs of the zodiac came from these different sources. The Ram for Aries, for instance came from Egypt, representing the god, Khnum. The Taurus bull originally came from Babylon, and the Capricorn goat came from Assyria.

Ancient Egypt had several gods and goddesses who took various forms, and ruled over all aspects of life. The functions of the gods represented earthly qualities, and god-virtues. The Egyptians also regarded certain animals as reflecting divine qualities. The unerring sight of the hawk (Horus) and the dynamic power of the bull (Apis) were examples of special animal qualities and symbols. It was believed that by embalming the animals, their mummies would preserve the divine qualities that influenced the culture in a positive way.

Another curious aspect of the gods and goddesses involved the combination of both human and animal into one god. There was a connection between the Egyptian Sphinx, The Greek Centaur and the Assyrian man-bull. They were dual creatures of human and animal for a reason. In all of the ancient mystery teachings, these creatures symbolized the dual nature of man, and suggested a hierarchy of celestial beings who had control of the destiny of humanity. The celestial beings were the twelve holy animals known as the constellations standing as symbols of impersonal spiritual emanations and energies. The Sphinx was a supreme guardian of the mysteries of the temples, denying entrance to the impious (some sources say this was a combination of Leo and Virgo); the centuar symbolized Sagittarius, the custodian of the knowledge of the secret doctrine; the Assyrian man-bull (Taurus) with five feet contained the wings of an eagle and the head of a man, signifying that the spiritual nature of man has wings, the head of a man and the body of a beast.

We will get into the genealogical relationship of the Egyptian pantheon of gods. However, some of them did not have a genealogical connection. One such god was Hapi, the god who represented the annual Nile flooding, which fertilized the land, an event that was paramount to the agricultural economy of Egypt. Hapi is known in one form as a Hippopotamus. Some sources suggest that the Hippopotamus may have symbolized the struggle against the evil god, Set and Horus, the divine god. Hippopotami were also sacred to Tauret, the divine midwife and goddess of pregnant women. Tauret (also called Taweret) had the head of a hippopotamus, the legs of a lion, the tail of a crocodile, and female breasts. This is what I love about Egyptian symbolism: I find it to be so rich, with vivid color and imagination.

One form of Hapi was a hermaphrodite: a strange, bearded creature which had the head of a hippopotamus, a fat belly, the huge genitals of a man, and massive breasts to give milk to everyone. (In the book, *The Story of Atlantis and the Lost Lemuria*, W. Scott-Elliot writes about the transition from the non-sexual reproduction to sexual reproduction of man. He states that sexual reproduction had been developed from the condition of hermaphroditism at a period of the organic history of the world during the evolution of the Third Root Race of man on Lemuria.)

In another form of deity, Hapi was a bodily form of a male-female figure, symbolic of bountiful fertility. Hapi often wore the clothes of a swamp fisherman with the colors of green and blue. This god/goddess was able to change genders, and to take on the shape of an animal at will. The Egyptians sang hymns of praise to Hapi, and erected shrines for each of the seven-mile stages into which they divided the Nile--which is 4,132 miles, the world's longest river. Thus we can see why the Nile had such influence on agriculture and worship.

The Egyptians depended on Hapi and the periodic flooding of the Nile which is his/her alter ego. He kept the land on both sides of the Nile fertile by scattering seeds into the water as it flowed out of the sluices (artificial channels for regulating the flow of water) onto the earth. Thus, Hapi was named the god of the Nile floods.

Another interesting god was Renenuter, known as, "Nourishing Snake," a local type of god of the harvest. Snakes were considered a positive symbol of wisdom in the Middle East. On a Roman marble relief dating from 100 A. D., Isis is shown leading a procession with a snake wrapped around her left arm, which was believed to bring good fortune. Additionally, the reason the Pharaohs had an asp at the middle of the forehead, was because it was a symbol that the Pharaoh-king had successfully passed the necessary initiations and training to enable him to raise the kundalini, or serpent energy, through all of the energy centers in the body. In our world today, we call these energy centers "chakras," a Sanskrit word.

Renenuter, who is also referred to as Renenet, was considered guardian of the pharaoh. As a cobra goddess, the gaze of Renenuter could terrify any enemy of the king.

Egyptian myths included those of local neighboring cultures combined with the generally known popular myths. Remnants of these myths are still alive in the Coptic and Muslim stories in many areas of Egypt, as well as the continent of Africa. A stone relief of Osiris and Isis from the Cushite culture in Ethiopia was found dating back to 700 B. C.

Research points to Ethiopia as a country that had strong connections to Egypt. For over 1600 years, the "Abuna," the bishop of Ethiopia, was appointed by the Patriarch of Cairo, Egypt. However, Emperor Haile Selassie changed that in 1959. Although the Orthodox Church of Ethiopia is a branch of the Coptic Church and intimate ties remain, it has been independent since 1959. A substantial percentage of the population of Ethiopia is Coptic, and follows the Alexandrian Coptic liturgy with one exception: it uses Geez, the ancient Ethiopian language, instead of the ancient Coptic language.

At one point in time, the Ark of the Covenant was moved from Egypt to Ethiopia. It had been found that the ark is the exact measurement of the sarcophagus that is in the King's Chamber in the Great Pyramid, and that it would have fit inside perfectly.

Speaking of Ethiopia, the Cushites and Hamites were connected to various nations of Africa including the ancient Egyptians and modern Berbers. The Hamites were descendants of Noah's son, Ham. As related in the book, *America B. C.,* by Barry Fell, Africans, Egyptians, and Libyans descended from Ham.

The stories at the core of mythology are based on things that happened in real life. Myths form a background for human behavior and motivation. They try to answer the questions of life, such as, "Why are we here?" Or, "Where do we go when we die?" Or, "Why do we go through the struggle of good and evil?" It is human nature to seek to know the meaning of life. Individuals want to know the answers to life's dilemmas, and will continue to seek to know that life is not meaningless, but accounts for something.

Most Egyptian myths were sustained until the end of the ancient Egyptian religion. From the first century A. D., the myths continued under the Coptic religion, a Christian religion that still exists in Egypt today. The Coptics are the only ones who have preserved the old Pharaonic language of ancient Egypt; they are now about 5% of the population in Egypt. The rest of Egypt practices Islam, with a very small showing of Judaism, mostly in Cairo. In 642 A. D., the myths came under the influence of Islam.

The word, "Copt," comes from the Greek word "Aigyptos," which was derived from "Hikaptah," a name for Memphis, the ancient capital of Egypt. Today, the word, Coptic, means Egyptian Christians, and the last stage of the Egyptian language script. It was Saint Mark, the Evangelist, who brought Christianity to Egypt in the first century during the reign of Nero, the Roman emperor. Tradition credits Mark, one of the disciples of Jesus who understood the deeper teachings of The Christ, with the founding of the Christian Church in Alexandria. Within 50 years of Saint Mark's arrival in Alexandria, Christianity had spread all over Egypt.

The sources of Egyptian myths were taken from The Pyramid Texts on the stone walls in the pyramid tombs of kings from the Fifth to the Eighth dynasties in Saqquara (Old Kingdom to First Intermediate Period). The Pyramid Texts are the oldest writings in Saqquara, Egypt, which is 19 miles from Cairo. (Doug Kenyon, whose magazine, "Atlantis Rising," includes information on ancient mysteries, believes that the Pyramid Texts were copied from an even older version.) Then we have the Coffin Texts of the Middle Kingdom, which were found inscribed on the coffins of nobles. Other sources were from the texts of kings and gods found in temples, such as the Temple of Osiris in Abydos.

Another fact that piqued my interest about Saqquara was that the first philosophy of spiritual guidance was practiced there. Once a year, a pilgrimage was made to the Step Pyramid at Saqquara. The purpose was to establish principles of human behavior and discipline. Here is where the present principle of Court Procedure was adopted. At this annual event, the Supreme Master of the pyramid would be enclosed in the sanctuary within this pyramid. The door was sealed with stone. However, one piece of stone had a hole in the center, enabling the Master to look through to view the people making the pilgrimage as they collected around the field outside. In order to enter the field, the pilgrims had to successfully enter a labyrinth of seven chambers. These seven chambers contained seven statues which stood for seven human activities: Spirit (power), Ego (thought), Body (action), Emotion (feeling), Intellect (mental power), Expression (unification), and Fulfillment (bliss).

When the pilgrims reached the last chamber of fulfillment, they climbed seven steps and entered into meditation. Then they took a final oath to bring forth a more positive pattern for the year ahead. This could have been the origin of the New Year's resolution. Upon taking this oath, the pilgrim entered the field of liberty, where he and the other pilgrims participated in the religious ceremony of rejoicing. Then the Supreme Master appeared from the inner chamber to bless the pilgrims before they returned to their various locations.

It takes a great deal of courage to embark on a book that includes the subject of astrology, especially if you want to approach the masses with it, because of the taboos that have been placed on this subject. But if you are earnest in learning the truth, you will find that all ancient religions had astrology (once considered sacred) as a part of the temple and ritual, be it astrology or astronomy. Because, as I have pointed out, they were one and the same.

Astrology is a master tool for understanding ourselves and the world through the language of symbols. Astrology is a collection of road signs...some are red lights; some are green lights, to help you along the path. Destiny often beckons you, such as when the Yod aspect appears in a chart, and it helps to have a map. The Yod aspect is "The Finger of God" aspect which denotes spiritual guidance and a soul destiny, through a "Y" formation in the natal chart. The Yod aspect lends itself to divine guidance and can help individuals find their purpose through the planets, signs and position in the natal chart. Even though one may not have a Yod aspect, there are other signposts in a natal chart that can point the way to a soul purpose.

It became clear to me how life-changing it can be for a person to know their soul purpose through charting horoscopes for clients. One client, whom I will call John, was extremely depressed after losing his job, and everything was going downhill. After doing his chart, I showed him that the "Finger of God" aspect was present in his chart. I explained how it pointed to a spiritual purpose in his life. This gave him a whole, new perspective, and today he is happy helping others as a counselor.

The Yod aspect can be calculated for a natal chart based on the exact time and place of birth. This aspect consists of two planets in a sextile aspect (which is sixty degrees) and when both planets are in a quincunx aspect (150 degrees) to a third planet, forming a "Y" position in the chart.

Astrology can be your triple A to help you reach your destination. It can help you to see the roadblocks or construction along the way. Astrology can help you to understand yourself better, to make better decisions, and to balance this with what is going on in the world. Astrology is based on natural life cycles, used for centuries to guide and inform. It can clear up misunderstandings and conflicts that are in the world scheme. We always need to remember that the stars impel, but they do not compel. We always have free will to make choices, but the stars can help to make the right, positive choices, especially amid our confusing times. And most of all, the study of Astrology can show where there is a spiritual purpose at work in our lives.

Another amazing fact: Every doctor takes the "Hippocratic Oath," because Hippocrates was the founding father of the medical profession. It has been found that he based his knowledge on astrology! He wrote in his diary that "He who practices medicine without the benefit of the movement of the planets and stars is a fool." When Hippocrates wrote: "Touch not with iron that part of the body ruled by the sign the Moon is transiting," it was evident that he knew something about astrology. For instance, if the Moon was in the sign of Gemini, the doctor would be careful of not touching the hands (since Gemini rules the hands) with an instrument made of iron. The Moon spends about two and a half days in each sign of the zodiac throughout one month.

Why am I explaining so much about astrology in this introduction? I never realized that astrology was such an important part of Egyptian mythology and culture until I traveled to Egypt. It was an integral part of their temples and art which had a hidden mystical nature. It was even taught in the Egyptian Mystery Schools.

I would like to close this introduction with a quote from Isabel Hickey, one of our most famous astrologers: "For centuries astrology fell into disrepute because, like so many things on earth, it fell into the wrong hands and was used as fortune telling and was exploited by those seeking to gain through it instead of seeking to give through it. The Light was withdrawn and the inner truths behind it were not given to the profane."

CHAPTER ONE

"I am Isis, mother of Horus. I invite you to take a walk with me through the wondrous land of Egypt. May the Light of the Eye of Horus guide you in discovering the hidden truths of our myths and symbols."

THE IMPORTANCE OF THE EYE

To the Egyptians, the eye was very important. The all-seeing eye is a significant symbol at the Great Pyramid of Giza. As the horizon of the Sun shines into the opening of the Great Pyramid, it is possible to see the symbol of an eye, which means "entrance," as well as knowledge. The Egyptian eye was an important symbol for the initiates as they studied life and metaphysical truths in the temples of Egypt.

There are several references to the Eye of Horus throughout Egyptian mythology. Sometimes it becomes intermingled with the eye of Rah, the original sun god. As you will see, there is always a challenge with conflicts in Egyptian lore. The Left Eye of Rah was the Sun, representing the sun god. The Right Eye of Horus was the Moon, and then it became represented as the Left Eye of Horus and the Right Eye of Horus. (In *The Book of Knowledge: The Keys of Enoch*, the Eye of Horus is described as a manifestation of the Eternal Eye through which the Father can create Light and physical creation.)

The Left Eye of Horus (Rah) represented the path of light, oneness with God, the positive side of life. The Right Eye of Horus represented the negative side of life that is overcome through worldly experience by using discernment and making wise decisions.

The Eye of Horus was considered "the Sacred Eye." The Sacred Eye was said to guide one on the road of darkness, and in tomb drawings, hovered over a dead man. The deceased was ushered into the Underworld by the Eye of Horus, accompanied by the mystical hands that held a bowl of flaming incense.

According to the myth concerning the phases of the Moon, the wicked god Set tore out the Eye of Horus. However, the eye was reconstructed by Thoth, the god of wisdom, becoming a symbol for articles that became lost, and then found again. Thereby, certain objects became more precious through the process of restoration. As a result, each part of the eye became a hieroglyphic symbol to represent the fraction that they used in measuring bushels of grain. The first half of the eye meant one-half of a bushel; the iris of the eye meant one-fourth of a bushel; the eyebrow meant one-eighth bushel; the other half of the eye meant one-sixteenth of a bushel; the swirl beneath the eye meant one-thirty-second of a bushel; and the appendage directly below the eye meant one-sixty-fourth of a bushel. After the fractions are combined together, the restored eye looks like Illustration One. Furthermore, when you total the fractional parts, you will see that the answer adds up to 63/64. What happened to the missing 1/64? It was allowed for the miraculous cement that would bring the injured eye back to life.

The Egyptians saw the six parts of the Sacred Eye as a well-rounded complete personification of the pharaoh who held both earthly and heavenly power within his grasp. And so it was the pharaoh who could shine through the Sacred Eye.

If you can understand the symbol of the Sacred Eye, the Oudjat, you can understand the quest for the ideal, perfect individual in the ancient Egyptian religion. The ideal individual was composed of six parts, as was the Sacred Eye. "Oudjat" means perfectly complete, with all parts accounted for. The Egyptians wore Sacred Eye amulets to insure that they could be whole with all faculties in perfect order. Therefore, let us remember that the Sacred Eye, one of the most mysterious of all Egyptian symbols, owed its shape and meaning to the sky god Horus. Some have even attributed the Milky Way, depicted as a giant falcon with wings outstretched, as the powerful Horus. William Henry, investigative mythologist, has much to say on this subject with a stargate twist. But that is another story.

Two important symbols were always found in the Egyptian tombs: Anubis and the Eye of Horus. Belongings of the dead were carried in boxes to the tomb and buried with the body. The belongings contained such items as clothing, furniture, jewelry and food. The boxes were decorated with the image of the Eye of Horus for the purpose of protection, and the image of Anubis to watch over them in the afterlife. (SEE ILLUSTRATION ONE, of the Eye of Horus referred to as the Wadjet Eye).

Illustration One: The Wadjet Eye (The Eye of Horus)

THE PRESENCE OF THE ZODIAC

In the research for my book, *Mystical Secrets of the Stars*, I was amazed to find that the ancient Hebrews had a huge representation of the Zodiac in an ancient temple, a fourth century synagogue, in Jerusalem, Israel, that was unearthed in 1932. A beautiful mosaic wheel of the zodiac depicted the twelve signs from Aries, the Ram, to Pisces, the Fish, in earthen tan, coral and brown colors, surrounded by a white tile design. Until this archeological find, it was thought that astrology was forbidden in the Jewish religion. But now we know that it was part of the Hebrew ancient synagogue worship, as is also evident in the temples of Egypt. This is only one of the clues that astrology was considered sacred at one time. It was interesting to learn that horoscopes were cast at birth in Egypt, and India, and that this practice was also a part of the Taoist religion in China.

In *The Book of Knowledge: the Keys of Enoch®*, by J. J. Hurtak, we are told that there is a special plan for humanity to be transformed, to rise to a higher universe, to rise to a higher consciousness in our bodies of light. After seeing my references to *The Keys of Enoch*, you may ask: Who is Enoch? We may remember that Enoch is in the Bible (Genesis 6:21) as the one who walked with God. Enoch was raised into heaven without going through death in his body of light. There is much detail in this book on how we can be part of the plan of resurrection. In Key 106, we are told that the twelve signs of the Zodiac are much more than most realize. The twelve signs of the Zodiac are referred to as "the Mazzaroth," the 12 threshold controls of the Zodiac used by the Brotherhood of Light. The Brotherhood of Light has the responsibility of preparing the physical and spiritual civilizations for the "new Jerusalem" (Revelation 21:1-5).

King Manasseh "built altars to all the starry hosts" (2 Kings 21:4-5). I found out that Herod, King of Judea from 37 B. C. - 4 A. D., utilized the zodiac, too. Interestingly enough, Herod was not a Jew by birth, but a descendant of the hated Edomites, as well as a member of the Idumean dynasty. When Herod rebuilt Solomen's Temple, the largest of all temples, he included a full replica of the Zodiac. He obviously was doing whatever he thought would find favor with the Jews.

It is a little-known fact that Abraham and Daniel, from the Bible, were astrologers. Benjamin Franklin, American statesman, author and inventor, was an astrologer to George Washington, American general and first president of the United States from 1789 to 1797. J. P. Morgan, U.S. financier, (1867-1943) used astrologers for his extremely successful financial activities.

One of the most renowned astrologers of all time was Cheiro. He became well known from the late 19th century to the early 20th century, when he entertained such famous people as Mark Twain, Teddy Roosevelt, Grover Cleveland and many other notables. President Cleveland's wife was so fascinated by Cheiro that she invited him to the White House to read her palm, and confirmed that Grover Cleveland believed in astrology. The most interesting part of this is that Cheiro believed that the occult secrets of the world came from the Egyptians, and that some day the secrets hidden in Egypt would be rediscovered. Cheiro warned Lord Carnarvon--months before he went to Egypt--not to open Tutankhamen's tomb. As it turned out, Cararvon died a short time after the opening of the site.

Henry Weingarten, Managing Director of the Astrologer's Fund Inc., uses astrology to pilot his businesses on Wall Street. The Astrologer's Fund employs astrology as its primary analysis tool to manage investment funds and advise worldwide investors and money managers. After a nearly successful attempt on the life of President Ronald Reagan in 1980, his wife, Nancy, sought the advice of astrologer Joan Quigley, convinced that she did not want to take chances on his safety without the guidance of a professional astrologer.

Today we know that astrology can be used as an important tool to help individuals see where they can be most successful in careers, in medical problems, love matters and ad infinitum. If astrology can be so helpful, then why did astrology get put down?

As religions became more organized in modern times, astrology became forbidden in the Western world. This was an attempt to take power and knowledge away from the masses, so that organized religion held more power and decided what the people should be taught. The esoteric knowledge found in astrology was definitely a threat to the controlled power of organized religion in later years. The reason is because astrology gives a cache of knowledge that can help an individual determine why he/she is here and what he/she can accomplish for soul growth. The religious authorities wanted people completely dependent on them and not to be able to advance in a spiritual way on their own. One of the greatest losses of esoteric knowledge was the disappearance of the forty-two books of Hermes during the burning of Alexandria, Egypt, because the Romans of that time and later the Christian leaders knew that these books must be eliminated before they could bring the Egyptians under their suppression. Fortunately, some volumes escaped the destruction and were buried in a location known only to certain initiates of the sacred schools.

Ironically, some of the early popes were hooked on astrology. Pope Julius II had the day for his coronation, and the day for his return from Germany, fixed by the astrologers. And Pope Paul III was reported never to have held a tribunal until his stargazers had fixed the hour. I personally know of a twentieth century monk who was given an assignment to study astrology for two years by his superiors. It is clear that religious scholars were very much into the study of astrology. In fact, the Vatican in Rome has a Secret Archive, a Historical Library, and a Papal Observatory. The library contains the largest collection of known astrological information in the world.

What is one of the tools that can help us remove the stumbling blocks of negative influence that plague our planet Earth? Barbara Marciniak, author of *Bringers of the Dawn*, said that astrology is a language and a whole spiritual opening. She said at a conference in Daytona Beach, Florida, in 1998, that the reason astrology is ridiculed to the public is because astrology is a major key to understanding where we are in evolution. Astrology gives you purpose. Astrology was hidden from people because it can help humanity understand why we are here and assist us in our spiritual growth. She said that there has always been an influence in the world that wants to control people. The more we mature spiritually, the less we are controlled by others. We are in the age of releasing limitations in order to enter into spiritual freedom. In order to do this, we need to know ourselves better. Our names, our birth dates, all have meaning, and astrology has been proven to work to help us obtain more knowledge of life.

Alice Bailey, in her esoteric writings, said that we need the knowledge of astrology in order to pass the initiations of life. At one level of soul initiation, which we all must pass someday, we are shown astrological symbols of the Zodiac, and we need to know what they mean in order to pass the initiation. (See Appendix of symbols.)

I found it interesting to learn that the great artist who hailed from Spain, Salvatore Dali, said that religion, art and science must be brought into harmony to work for humanity. This is what the Egyptians believed. This is the age when it will be possible. It is up to us to bring about harmony in religion, art and science with our minds, thoughts and attitudes.

There is much debate as to whether astrology came from the Kabbalah, the ancient mystic Hebrew writings, or the ancient Egyptian teachings of the mystery schools. The second branch of the Kabbalah explains the planet Uranus in great detail. To the ancient Greeks, Uranus was the personification of Heaven. Also in Hermetic astrology, the ancient Egyptian astrology, there is considerable understanding of the planet Uranus, while it was not officially discovered until March 13, 1781, by Sir William Herschel. This poses a historical dilemma.

Through Hermetic astrology, coming from Greek and Egyptian cultures, we are taught that the soul is the channel through which experience is assimilated and character is built. Here we learn that the natal birth chart is the map of the soul. Each soul enters into existence to fulfill a specific purpose in society. During certain periods, the soul is given a glimpse of the glorious potentials that are possible.

After my travels to Egypt, I was especially surprised by all of the symbols of astrology in the temples. This led me to dig more deeply for evidence of the Egyptian version of astrology. While they followed some of the symbols of the Babylonian astrology, they also had their own

Egyptian meaning for the astrological periods of the year. Moreover, I found their timing of the months slightly different, due to the following of the yearly cycle of the Nile River, instead of the Roman calendar.

Another thing struck me. It was always assumed that the Egyptians worshipped the Sun. But I found out that the ancients did not actually worship the physical Sun. They had knowledge of the Almighty Source of all Life, who resided in the Great Central Sun, beyond the Sun. The Great Central Sun is spiritual rather than physical, like many creations in the Cosmos. The Great Central Spiritual Sun is the source from which all life was born, the Universal First Cause.

Modern science confirms that there are many galaxies with a central sun in the universe. The sun was a symbol of God. As time went on, some Egyptians attached their own meaning to it.

During the course of Egyptian history, several attempts were made to restrict the number of gods. However, this effort was highly opposed by the priests, because their importance hinged on the people believing in various gods. It was not only the importance of the station of the priests, but the money that was made, as well. At one time there were more than a thousand gods. The more gods, the more money the priests made.

THE PHARAOH WHO BROUGHT BACK THE BELIEF IN ONE GOD

One of the bravest attempts to restrict the number of gods was made by Amenhotep IV, King of Upper and Lower Egypt, from the Eighteenth dynasty. This king changed his name from Amenophis IV, to Akhenaten, and tried to bring back an ancient original meaning of God. As a young pharaoh, he learned to honor the everlasting spirit within, called "The Sun behind the sun."

Akhenaten's sense of this everlasting light spurred him on to establish a new social order to reinstate the ancient teachings. Realizing the cosmic meaning of the Sun as the Universal Father, he was able to establish a true brotherhood of light, although it was only for a short time of sixteen years. Thirteen hundred years before the birth of Christ, this spiritual pharaoh applied the principles of democracy, women's suffrage, and arbitration to settle internal conflicts. Akhenaten declined to go to war against enemies of Egypt because, in his belief, all were children of the sun and his brothers. Therefore, the gods were displaced with a universal concept; God was a Universal Essence, instead of a tribal god. In fact, he built a temple dedicated to the Formless One. The Solar Disc was chosen as the symbol of the Universal Force. The light of the Sun was the giver of life to the people, and this is depicted in drawings representing Akhenaten. This unusual pharaoh sacrificed wealth, position, honor and his life rather than lower his ethical, spiritual values. This king's vision of a government based upon the principles of love for humanity is still elusive.

Akhenaten rejected all of the gods except for Aten, who was considered the solar god and the only source of life. However, the decadent priesthood had much more influence during that time (1378 - 1362 B. C.), and resisted the attempt of honoring just one God (monotheism) by having Akhenaten killed. During this time, the Egyptian priesthood had become a magical cult, referred to as "Black Magicians."

The throne then went to his son, Smekh-ka-Re, who only reigned for three years and died. Then the throne passed to the next son, Tutankhamun, who was only ten years old, and a puppet for the priesthood. After Tutankhamun died at only 18 years old, the throne went to Ay, a priest of Maat, and vizier. Ay and Har-em-hab, husband of Ay's daughter, now had control so that they could reinstate the polytheistic gods that they wanted the people to worship. The worship of Aten was abolished, and the worship of Amun, along with other gods, was reinforced. This stands as a good example of politics, even back then.

I was very upset when I saw what they did to the statue of Tutankhamun at the Temple of Luxor. It must have been a beautiful statue of Tutankhamun and his young wife, but it had been severely smashed. Many of the statues of Akhenaton and his family were also defaced, and his temples were obliterated.

Hamid Bey, the founder of the Coptic Fellowship in America, said that the ancient Egyptians believed in one God. They believed that the human entity could never be destroyed, but that the soul becomes detached for different lifetimes. To the Egyptians, the consciousness of living was never lost. The passing away of the physical body does not take away the mental body of the individual; rather, it lives on in consciousness. I will go more into how they were given the teachings of the Brotherhood of Light, under the subject of Serapis.

CHAPTER TWO

WHAT WE KNOW FROM HISTORY

If we go with historical data, we first see credit for discovering astrology to the Chaldean priests, going back in time to Ashurbanipal, King of Assyria, 669 BC to 626 BC. This was due to the translations of written cuneiform tablets in the library of King Ashurbanipal. However, horoscopes have been discovered as far back as 4200 B. C. in Egypt, with charts cast in rectilinear tables, dividing the sky into twelve parts, each given a name and a figure. Our present day calendar is based on ancient Egyptians, who were the first to adopt a solar calendar in 4241 B. C., noted as the earliest "accepted" event date in history.

Evidence was found that the priests of Babylon used watchtowers to make maps of the skies; in addition, clay tablets were discovered that recorded accurate motions of the sun and moon going back to 3800 B. C.

In the second millennium B. C. Abraham emigrated from Ur, a prominent city of the Sumerians. The Sumerians were regarded as Chaldeans by the Hebrews. The Chaldeans took over Mesopotamia in 606 B. C., according to Herodatus. The Chaldean priests were the new Babylonians who were known for developing astrology.

The Persians conquered Babylon in 538 B.C., and the Persian priesthood were called "Magi," which meant master astrologers. The incidence of a star guiding the Three Magi to Bethlehem was an undeniable astronomical event.

Let me preface the following Egyptian chronology by saying that there is no precise agreement as to the date of the official start of the dynastic periods. Various sources range from 4056 B. C. to almost 2850 B. C. for the beginning of the dynastic history. I have seen slightly different dates for each period, but these are the most logical that I have found.

With this in mind, let us consider the timetable of ancient Egypt:

From 4500 to 3050 B. C. was deemed the Pre-dynastic Period.

From 2920 - 2575 B. C. was the early Dynastic period of the First to Third Dynasties.

From 2575 - 2175 B. C. was the Old Kingdom and the Fourth to the Sixth Dynasties.

From 2175 - 1975 B. C. was the First Intermediate period which represented the Seventh to Eleventh dynasties.

From 1975 - 1640 B. C. was The Middle Kingdom, representing the Twelfth to the Thirteenth dynasties.

From 1640 - 1539 B. C. was the Second Intermediate Period of the Fourteenth to Seventeenth dynasties.

From 1539 - 1292 B. C. was the period of the Early New Kingdom, representing the Eighteenth dynasty.

From 1292 - 1075 B. C. was the Late New Kingdom, representing the Nineteenth to Twentieth dynasties.

From 1075 - 715 B. C. was the Third Intermediate Period which represented the Twenty-first to Twenty-third dynasties.

From 715 - 332 B. C. was the Late Period representing the Twenty-fourth to the Thirty-first dynasties.

From 332 B. C. to 395 A. D. became the Greco-Roman Period.

I am going to highlight those periods and events that are most relevant for our purposes. The following is what I have pieced together for the most important events of certain periods:

The parade of pharaohs ended with the conquest of Alexander (III) the Great in 332 B. C. The Ptolemies ruled from 332 to 30 B. C. Soter Ptolemy I (367 - 283 B. C.) was born in Macedonia, Greece, and was the founder of the Macedonian dynasty in Egypt and the first of the Ptolemies.

Philadelphus Ptolemy II (309 - 247 B. C.), son of Ptolemy I, was king of Egypt from 285 B. C. to 247 B. C.

Cleopatra was the last of the Ptolemies to rule under the Greek period. She was Macedonian and Iranian. Her relationships with Julius Caesar and Mark Antony postponed the fall of Egypt to Rome. Julius Caesar (100 - 44 B. C.), along with his generals, Crassus and Pompey, formed the First Triumvirate in 60 B. C., which made Caesar immortal in the Gallic Wars. As Caesar governed with wisdom, this era was a great period in Roman history. His assassination in 44 B. C. produced anarchy, from which the Second Triumvirate emerged with Octavian, Antony and Lepidus. Octavian was Caesar's nephew and heir, making him the true successor.

Cleopatra and Antony were defeated at Actium in 31 B. C. After their suicides, Egypt came under Roman rule by Octavian, who received the title of "Augustus," which meant the real ruler, or "Imperator." He was considered the first Roman emperor. His rule began the period of peace of 200 years, referred to as the "Pax Romana."

Sometime between 31 B .C. and 14 A. D., Egypt was invaded by the Nubians, who came from the south. The Romans defeated them, overtook their capital, Napata, and opened a trading center south of Aswan. It became a significant trading center between Rome and India.

Claudius Ptolemaeus (127 - 151 A. D.) was a Greek mathematician and astronomer at Alexandria, Egypt. He was called Ptolemy, and invented the Ptolemaic Astronomical System, where the earth was the fixed center of the universe, with the heavenly bodies rotating around it. This system was later modified by other astronomers.

THE MAN CALLED "THE SLEEPING PROPHET"

Edgar Cayce was a man who became known as "the Sleeping Prophet" for his ability to go into trance to receive information for individuals needing healing and to draw information from what has been called the "Akashic records." Before I go into what the Akashic records actually are, let me give you some background on Edgar Cayce because during his readings, he gave extensive information on Egypt.

In May, 1976, I traveled to Virginia Beach, Virginia, to find out more about the intriguing Edgar Cayce. I attended a conference given by the Association for Research and Enlightenment, often called A. R. E. Since the conference was such an enjoyable and awakening experience, I became a member immediately and began attending conferences at Virginia Beach almost every year.

Within the A. R. E. Center at 215 67th Street in Virginia Beach, is a fascinating library which is the most extensive esoteric library in the United States. This library contains over 14,000 readings given by Edgar Cayce as recorded by his secretary, Gladys Davis. Now, you may be asking, what is an Edgar Cayce reading?

Cayce would put himself into a self-induced trance where he made contact with the universal mind. People who had health problems, sometimes labeled "incurable" by the doctors, went to Cayce for help. His clients did not have to be physically present with him. All Cayce needed to give a person a reading was their name and where they lived. Cayce then often prescribed age-old remedies, such as herbs or castor oil packs which were health remedies of early America, but became forgotten as effective remedies. The clients of Cayce who followed his directions were cured, according to the readings. As Cayce became well-known for this invaluable gift, the number of readings increased. However, as time went on, the information was no longer limited to physical or medical information. Cayce began to receive information on how the health problems of clients were related to a past lifetime, and what they could do in this lifetime to solve the problem. This expansion of information was strange to Cayce upon awakening from his trance reading, because until these occurrences, he did not believe in the theory of reincarnation, that we have lived in lifetimes before the present one. Also, while in trance, Cayce often spoke in foreign languages which he could not speak in the conscious state. Cayce made his transition to the spirit side of life in 1945, leaving a great legacy of information. And one of his caches of knowledge had to do with the Akashic records.

The Akashic records are vibrations recorded of everything that has happened in life throughout the ages. In Edgar Cayce reading, 1020-17, he said that the Wise Men, The Magi, had studied records of ancient wisdom kept in Egypt. And from these records, they came to know about the time of the Messiah and the Essenes, a Jewish sect whose purpose was to prepare for the event of the coming of the Messiah. The thirteen papyrus books found in Nag Hammadi, Egypt in 1945, as well as the Dead Sea Scrolls, discovered later, are considered to be the source of information to which Edgar Cayce was referring.

In reading 2067-1, Cayce says that much of the information relating to the Essenes and the Wise Men were lost in the burning of the Alexandrian library. Nevertheless, some portions may have survived in the Vatican Library, or other surprising places, such as the underground library at the Serapeum in Alexandria, Egypt.

Egypt was divided into Upper Egypt (the south which was secluded by the desert, and the cataracts of the Nile), and Lower Egypt (the north which opened to world trade through the Mediterranean Sea). The entire country of Egypt needed strong control. The religion of the Pharaohs provided the beliefs to hold this vast area together. Whenever circumstances commanded it, the Egyptian religion and beliefs were altered. Perhaps this is one explanation of why there are discrepancies or changes in the way the gods are represented.

It was about 3000 B. C. when Upper and Lower Egypt became unified. And with this came an increase in the number of ways that the gods were depicted. Pictorial images from this period show the pharaoh with animals as symbols of power or certain qualities, as well as assisting with activities of hunting or war.

In the following chapters you will be given inside information on how the most popular and effective gods were characterized.

CHAPTER THREE

"Re is more than the sun-god; he is the universe, the sole god who has made himself for eternity."

--Akhenaten, King of Upper and Lower Egypt

THE PANTHEON OF GODS

The word, "Pantheon," actually means "collection." In *The Hathor Material* by Virgina Essene and Tom Kenyon, we are told that the Egyptian Pantheon is a representation of force fields that move through the universe. It is recommended that when you contemplate the pantheon of gods, to remember that the literal understanding of it was given to lesser minds of the period. All teachings were given on multiple levels of understanding. What was understood on the literal level by the less evolved minds, was understood by the high priests and initiates on a higher level as symbolic of energies, in other words, force fields that moved.

The pantheon of gods is an aspect of the One Creative Force of All That There Is. The gods are streams of consciousness that radiate from the One Source. These deities are positive forces with which initiates were taught to align, while not forgetting that the Creator was the one pure Source. The Egyptian religion was not just a cult of many gods worshipped by the common people; it was much more than that. The Egyptian Pantheon was originally made up of forty-two spiritual beings who came to be called the "neteru," which meant powerful forces. Each neter had a region in Egypt where rituals were conducted at a temple honoring a specific god. Moreover, each neter had a corresponding star to which the "ka," the etheric double, was linked, providing a transcendent communication with something that was found to be greater than the physical self. (This is similar to what is referred to as the "Overself Body" in *The Book of Knowledge: The Keys of Enoch* ® by J. J. Hurtak.) All Egyptian temples followed a structural pattern which enabled a sacred experience. This included numbers, time, geometry and volume. The method of transcending human life into divine life was through transformation, which was a technology based in what was labeled "magic." Egyptologists confirm that all of the temples are aligned with a star system. For example, the Temple of Horus at Edfu was aligned with Canopus, and the Queen's Chamber in the Great Pyramid at Giza was aligned with Sirius.

I found it interesting that Egyptian mythology is similar to the teachings of the Brotherhood of Light, in that each male has a complementary counterpart, known as Twin Flames or soul mates. The male god, together with the female goddess, makes up the complete whole of the one Fire Being from which they were created. The male god and female goddess each have qualities and assignments that weave together in their purpose in life. A prime example of this is Osiris and Isis, as you will see as we go on.

The chart of Egyptian gods begins with Rah, the begetter of all gods. The great god, Rah, represented the Sun. (SEE ILLUSTRATION TWO.) Originally, he was called Re (pronounced Ray) and later it became Ra, pronounced Rah. I am going to use this latter form because it is the most popular. Rah was the highest god and traveled the sky in his sun boat. The Sun god took three forms: One was in the morning, as the beetle Khepri, called, "He who comes into existence." The second form was during mid-day, as the falcon-headed Rah. The third form was the evening setting sun, the human-headed Aten, "He who is complete."

Illustration Two: Rah

As a powerful deity, Rah controlled all life and was associated with the ruling kings, or pharaohs, who were considered the Sons of Rah.

The Egyptian astrology, Hermetic astrology, is based on a central solar system with the planets revolving around the sun. This astrology teaches that the soul gathers experience in order to build character, and that the birth chart is the map of the soul. Each soul enters earth life in order to fulfill an important role. A glorious possibility awaits those who can realize his/her soul purpose. Astrology can point the way.

The wife of Amun-Rah was Mut, the mother-goddess, represented as a woman with a double crown. Their son was Khonsu, called "the Traverser." He was merciless in his pursuit of the enemies of the gods. Khonsu was the first Moon god. These three made up the Egyptian Trinity.

Then there was Ptah and Sekhmet, who gave birth to their son, the lotus god, Nefertum. Nefertum represented the lotus from which the sun rose after the birth of the world. Ptah, Sekhmet and Nefertum formed a divine triad. Nefertum protected the eastern border of Egypt. He had a lion's head, surmounted by a lotus flower with two feathers sprouting from it.

Next, we have Khnum, the creator god, and Neith, his wife, a warrior-headed goddess who carried arrows and a shield.

Shu is the god of emptiness. He shares his reign with Geb, his son, as King of the Earth. Tefnut is his wife, who is called The Eye of Rah. She personifies moisture, as goddess of moisture. Along with Shu, she separates heaven and earth. Here is where there is some confusion. Hathor is said to be the daughter of Rah and Mut. Then Tefnut is said to be the daughter of Rah and Mut. Are they one and the same, or are they different? This is one of the dilemmas I mentioned earlier with which we have to deal in this wonderful puzzle from the ancient past.

Geb is god of the earth, and son of Shu and Tefnut. His wife is Nut, goddess of the sky and part of the god of the ocean. Nut is depicted as an arch across the heavens, bending over her husband, Geb. Geb and Nut are the parents of Osiris, Isis, Set and Nephthys.

Osiris is son of Geb and Nut. His consort (wife) is Isis, and their son is Horus.

Horus and Hathor are husband and wife, and begot the Child Moon god, Ihy, also called Harsomtus.

Thoth, god of wisdom, was later associated with the Moon, but he also represented Mercury, while Venus was represented by Hathor.

Egyptian gods were often combined to form a new deity with different functions. The first part of the deity's name represented the chief characteristic of the god, while the added name referred to a specific feature of the god, which varied from time to time, according to the territory of Egypt in which the god was honored. For example, Rah-Shu described the Sun god as the separator of sky and earth by means of a god of solar light. Next, Shu-Onuris gave meaning to Shu as the "Bringer of the Distant One—Retriever of the Solar Eye." The Solar Eye was the distant lioness Sehkmet, who angrily left her position at the forehead of Rah.

Sehkmet-Tefnut-Hathor-Bastet was the complete personality of the Solar Eye in its four different aspects. Each of these four different names is a word of power, which lived on after many of the old gods lost their popularity. In later Egyptian art, Isis merges with Hathor. One example of this confusion is when I went into a store to buy a statue of Hathor, it was catalogued on their computer as Isis. (SEE ILLUSTRATION THREE, one version of Sehkmet)

Illustration Three: One version of Sekhmet

Bastet was the aspect of the gentle cat goddess of the region of Bubastis. Located north of Cairo, Bubastis was once the capital of Egypt, around 950 B. C. Bastet was also considered the daughter of the Sun god who represented the power of the Sun to ripen crops. As a goddess of pleasure and fertility, she became one of the most popular deities, in that colorful festivals were celebrated in her honor at her temple in Bubastis. The worshippers of Bastet made many statues of her in order to placate the goddess. In ancient Egypt, cats were venerated as animals sacred to Bastet. In fact, in honor of Bastet, all cats in Egypt were thought sacred and often mummified when they died. Some were even buried with their masters. The Egyptian name for the house cat was "miu." (SEE ILLUSTRATION FOUR.)

Certain animals were held sacred among the ancient nations because of a certain sensitivity to the astral fire. The cat is an excellent example of this sensitiveness, since it is a magnetized animal. If you would just observe yourself stroking the fur of a cat in a dark room, you will be able to see the electrical emanations in the form of a green phosphorescent light. In the temples of Bastet, three-colored cats were venerated (such as the calico cat), as well as those cats who had two eyes of a different color. The Magicians of the Middle Ages surrounded themselves with cats, snakes, bats and monkeys, simply because the Magicians were able to borrow the power of the astral light from these animals and use it for their own purposes. This is why the Egyptians kept cats in the temples, and the Greeks kept serpents for the oracles of Delphi.

Illustration Four: Bastet

FAVORITE EGYPTIAN MYTHS

I found it so intriguing that there were various myths expressing similar concepts of the gods, but yet different. Therefore, I would like to present some of these varieties so that the reader can get a deeper picture of the myths that have taken hold.

Author Joseph Campbell, considered the foremost authority on mythology, stated that in the creation myths the soul is looking for a way of experiencing the transcendent power that can open within us, giving us the power to transcend ego in such a unique way. Many of the gods were seen as heroes. In his famous book, *The Hero with a Thousand Faces,* Campbell demonstrates how the journey of consciousness forms the basis of the myth of the hero, or the myth of the human soul. Humanity needs heroes—someone who has chosen to sacrifice an aspect of their lives to something that is bigger than self. In other words, a hero is an individual who has found a way to transcend ego for a higher cause.

Can you think of a modern day hero or heroine? I can. The first one that comes to mind is Mother Teresa, who has been canonized a saint. How many of us could set aside our comforts of life to walk the streets of India and help the poorest of the poor…the lowest of the low society in life? It certainly takes a heroine effort. We know that Mother Teresa's life was not an easy one. Yet she found a way to transcend it all for a higher power, and, in that respect, she is a goddess. Think of how many individuals she helped. Think of those individuals who had the opportunity through her to raise their consciousness to something higher than they could ever experience alone. It was done through love, pure love of humanity. She must have had a divine connection.

In mythology and in primitive logic, there is always an element of synchronicity between what happens in the sky of the outer world and what happens in the heart of humanity. The sun's yearly drama of death and rebirth reflects a process taking place within the individual. This is the foundation of the principles of astrology, and is why it has persisted throughout many thousands of years.

Here are some of the Egyptian heroes and myths.

THE CREATION MYTH

In ancient Egypt, creation myths took various forms.

One myth begins with the god Ptah, who was worshipped approximately 3,000 B. C. in Memphis, Egypt. (In *The Book of Knowledge: The Keys of Enoch,* Ptah is mentioned as a Cosmic being who serves under Archangel Michael on the Throne of God. He is referred to as "Creator Lord of Life, father of fathers." One of his purposes is to qualify civilizations for spiritual education of the soul.)

In the myth Ptah found himself in the primordial waters where he used thought and speech to produce the eight divinities called Ogdoad. Ogdoad consisted of: god Kuk and goddess Kauket, representing darkness; god Huh and goddess Hauhet, representing infinity; god Amun and goddess Amaunet, representing hidden power; and god Nun and goddess Naunet, representing the watery abyss.

Another myth claims that the four male and female divine pairs of the Ogdoad were the creators of the primeval waters. In some Ogdoad myths, these gods and goddesses are portrayed as snake-headed goddesses, frog-headed gods, and so forth, to emerge together to form the mythic Cosmic Egg, giving birth to the sun god, Rah.

This myth originated from Heliopolis, Egypt: The creator god, Atum, emerged from the primitive ocean. He created duality from his own seed. He poured the seed into his mouth and spat out his children in the form of the twins, Shu, the god of air, and Tefnut, the lioness from the solar disk, also called the goddess of moisture. This couple, Shu and Tefnut, begot Nut, the goddess who personifies the sky, and Geb, who personifies the earth and is leader of the gods. Geb and Nut were parents of the gods of the "Osiris cycle" (Osiris, Isis, Set, Nephthys and Horus). As oldest son, Osiris was next in line to become king of the gods. Osiris and Isis became the royal couple. Isis personifies the royal throne and the star Sirius. Osiris was often shown as a mummified god, as he became ruler of the underworld (heaven), manifesting as the constellation of Orion. Brother Set was born next, who is identified with the Big Dipper constellation. His consort was his sister, Nephthys.

The nine deities known as Atum, Shu, Tefnut, Geb, Nut, Set, Neththys, Isis, and Osiris were collectively called the "Ennead," which is derived from a Greek word meaning "nine." All of these nine deities were the first nine gods of Heliopolis, and were divine. However, one was human as well as divine, and that was Osiris, the god who was murdered, renewed, and resurrected to become the god of the underworld, as heaven was called by the Egyptians.

THE OSIRIS MYTH

This myth describes the constant struggle for power. Should the throne go to the son or the brother of the deceased king? This myth also deals with death and resurrection, and the cycle of life. Osiris came to symbolize the Nile River, the fertile part of Egypt. Set, his brother, symbolized the dry, desert wasteland. This myth gave great meaning to the afterlife. Thereby, it gave Egyptians an association with Osiris. Those who passed into spirit and had proved their merit with the weighing of the heart, could follow Osiris through the Duat in the sky and became resurrected. Osiris gave the Egyptians the hope of an afterlife in the underworld (our heaven). More is given about the hidden knowledge of Osiris later in Chapter Seventeen.

THE MYTH OF THE AFTERLIFE AND HELL

The creators of myths have been busy at work on the question of what happens to us after we die. There is much agreement that existence continues after so-called death but in another place, or on another plane. The belief of the Egyptians was that the soul, which had just passed into spirit, entered the "Hall of Double Justice" to meet Osiris, god of the dead. Osiris was joined by Anubis, god of embalming, and Thoth, Scribe of the Underworld. Also presiding were forty-two judges, representing the forty-two provinces of Egypt, as well as the forty-two parts of the human conscience. Presented before Osiris, Anubis and Thoth, the deceased person's heart was placed on one side of a calibrated scale, and a feather was placed on the other side. The feather is a symbol of the goddess Maat, representing truth and justice. If the heart weighed heavier than the feather, Am-mit, eater of the dead, devoured the soul of the deceased. Am-mit is an unsavory monster that is part lion, part hippopotamus and part crocodile. In order to help the soul from being devoured, the relatives of the deceased often made offerings to Osiris, to be buried with the necessary amulets. If the heart and the feather were perfectly balanced, the deceased enjoyed bliss in the afterlife. Then there was the belief that in the afterlife, work had to be accomplished, such as the maintenance of canals and cataracts, and the control of the waterfalls along the Nile. In order to insure that the deceased would relax in the afterlife, the departed were buried with small statuettes that were supposed to carry out the work for them.

THE RAMSES MYTH

One myth has it that Ramses II established the four cardinal signs of the Zodiac which are Aries, Cancer, Libra and Capricorn. Ramses was one of the most famous pharaohs of Egypt, who practiced astrology and lived a long life. His 67-year reign (1290 to 1223 B. C.) was one of the longest in the history of Egypt. When he died in 1223 B. C., his body was laid in a sarcophagus in the Temple of Karnak at Thebes (now Luxor.) His tomb was purposely built so that the rays of the sun would touch into it at a special date. (Speaking of the longevity of Ramses II, I ran across some information that struck me like a thunderbolt. Laurence Gardner, who is a fellow of the Society of Antiquities of Scotland, A Knight Templar of Saint Anthony and author of *Top Ten Bloodlines of the Holy Grail*, offered some tantalizing information. He said that the Egyptians and Israelites used a mysterious white powder derived from gold which had magical powers and esoteric properties. This powder increased the longevity of the pharaohs, as well as their perceptive ability. It changed them physically, making them glow, and because of this were called "the shining ones." This magical powder, called "mfkzt," was associated with the power of levitation. It was also used to power the Ark of the Covenant, which had the potential of being used as a battlefield weapon.)

MYTH OF THE ORIGIN OF THE IMPERFECT STATE OF THE WORLD AND THE COSMIC CYCLE.

As the myth goes, the angry Solar Eye goddess, Sekhmet, was sent to earth to destroy humanity because people no longer respected her father, Rah, the sun god. But then Rah felt compassion for humanity, thereby needing to fool the bloodthirsty goddess and to change the plan. He arranged for the Earth to be flooded with red-colored beer. When the goddess reached earth, she thought the world was covered in blood. She anxiously drank it, and became intoxicated and happy, transforming her into the gentle cat known as Bastet. Somehow, Rah was not entirely satisfied. So he visited the heavenly Nut, and created the cosmos. He patterned the stars in the sky, formed Nut to make an arch over Geb, with the support of Shu, and assigned Thoth, the Moon god, as his representative of the sun at night.

THE BENU BIRD MYTH

The Benu Bird was depicted on the walls of Egyptian tombs as a blue heron (SEE ILLUSTRATION FIVE). The Egyptian name, Benu, means "the Ascending One." An ancient Egyptian myth states that the Benu Bird had risen from the waters of life from the beginning of time. Although considered a legend, the ancients deemed the Benu a reality. In *The Book of Knowledge: the Keys of Enoch®* by J. J. Hurtak, the Benu is described as a Phoenix vehicle for resurrection from the physical world, working with the Cherubim and Seraphim angels. At Heliopolis he was worshipped as the soul of Osiris. On the other hand, he was connected with the cult of Rah, the sun god. Here Rah took on a secondary form as the Benu and was worshipped at the temples of Atum and Rah. As a symbol of rebirth, the Benu Bird created itself. The Greeks associated the Benu with the Phoenix Bird that was the shape and size of an eagle. The Greek version of a self-creating bird was the Phoenix that rose from its own ashes every 500 years. One legend has the Phoenix Bird born from the depths of Arabia after which he flew to the temple of Heliopolis with the body of his father where the Phoenix buried him after coating him with myrrh.

Illustration Five: The Benu Bird

THE EGYPTIAN/GREEK/ROMAN MYTH OF AMUN

It was acknowledged that the Egyptians considered Amun as the highest deity, after which he was called Zeus by the Greeks, and Jupiter Ammon by the Romans. Amun could create by his will, and thus created Kneph and Athor, male and female, which represented the separation of the sexes. In this myth, Kneph and Athor produced Osiris and Isis. From this story, Osiris was worshipped as the god of sun, warmth, and fertility. Osiris was also viewed as god of the Nile and visited his earthly wife, Isis, when the Nile spilled over onto the earth, whereby Isis represented the Earth. Here, the god, Serapis was considered the same as Osiris. These gods were accompanied by Anubis, who was considered a guardian dog with a head of a jackal, or an Egyptian form of dog, symbolic of eternal faithfulness. In this myth, Horus, the son of Osiris, is depicted as Harpocrates, seated on a lotus flower with his finger to the side of his lips.

In Moore's "Irish Melodies," he gives reference to Harpocrates:
"Thyself shall, under some rosy bower,
sit mute, with thy finger on thy lip;
Like him, the boy, who born among
the flowers that on the Nile-stream blush,
Sits ever thus,--his only song
To Earth and Heaven, "Hush all, Hush!"

THE MYTH OF THE SPHINX

Down through the centuries, sandstorms have continued to threaten the Sphinx, and at one time the Great Sphinx was buried in sand up to the neck, with only the head above ground. A legendary story grew that, during that period, Egyptians would stand next to its lips to receive guidance and wisdom. In approximately 1400 B. C., a prince who had been hunting, happened to stop to rest near the Sphinx. Exhausted, he fell asleep and had a dream. In this dream he heard the Sphinx speak to him. The voice promised to make him king of Egypt, even though he had older brothers, if he would clear the sand away from its body. After he woke up and contemplated the dream, he was determined that he would do just that. After he ascended to the throne as Pharaoh Thutmose IV, he accomplished the feat of clearing away the sand from the Sphinx.

THE MYTH OF THE LORD OF THE NILE

Approximately 4,600 years ago, the pharaoh Zoser ruled Egypt. The Egyptians believed that the pharaohs were gods, and that they would join Rah to travel with him in the Boat of the Sun. It was important for the pharaoh to build a tomb to preserve his body, because without a preserved body, it was believed the soul would die. Zoser perceived that the brick tombs of former pharaohs would not be everlasting. Therefore, he instructed his visier, Imhotep, to build a tomb that would outlast the ravages of time. Imhotep created a mastaba, a tomb of stone, of one step of stone upon another, which became the Step Pyramid, the first known pyramid.

In the eighteenth year of the reign of Zoser, the Egyptians were faced with a disaster. The yearly flooding of the Nile did not come about, and all growing crops perished. Zoser temporarily fed the people from granaries that had surplus of the harvest of past years. But after seven years, the supply was exhausted. He called upon Imhotep, the wise one, to help him out of this dilemma, since the people were demanding that this pharaoh use his god-like powers to save the people. When Zoser questioned Imhotep on how to find the god or goddess of the Nile to bring life back to the country, Imhotep said he would need to go to the Temple of Thoth at Hermopolis to find the sacred books to learn what to do.

Several days passed before Imhotep returned with an answer. He told Zoser that he needed to seek the mystery of the Nile to the south on the island of Abu, the City of the Beginning, the first dry land that arose from the waters of Nu. "This is where Rah spoke the names of all things created. There is a cave where the river rests and is reborn every year. With new strength, it rushes forth through two caverns, symbolizing the breasts that nourish the land of Egypt. The lord of this cave is Khnum, the Lord of the Nile. He is the only one who can make the Nile flood again."

Thereupon, Zoser sailed on his royal barge to Abu, the birthplace of the Nile. He entered the Temple of Khnum and bowed before his altar, offering bread, beer, geese and oxen, known to please the gods. Then a figure appeared, with the head of a ram and wide horns. He addressed Zoser: "I am Khnum, Lord of the Nile, who strikes the earth with my sandals to flood the land to feed the people of Egypt."

Zoser asked: "Lord of the Nile, how have I offended you that you have not sent the flood for seven years?"

The reply came: "Why does the Pharaoh build a tomb so splendid, but neglect the gods? You must restore honor to the gods before the Nile will rise again."

Zoser promised that it would be done. He commissioned Imhotep to build a special temple to Khnum, to be filled with gold, silver, copper and lapis lazuli, per Khnum's request. Then, once again, the Nile overflowed its banks, yielding the rich mud to help the crops grow. This was a lesson that the wealth of Egypt was the gift of the Lord of the Nile. (Imhotep, who was high priest of Heliopolis, was actually revered throughout the ancient world. Not only was he known as a genius for building the first pyramid, he was elevated to the status of a god, which was quite unusual for someone who was not a pharaoh. The tomb of Imhotep drew hordes of people in need of healing, because legend had it that he healed pilgrims visiting his burial site at Saqquara.)

CHAPTER FOUR

INTRIGUING MYSTERIES

Egypt is a land of surprises as well as mysteries. This country is ruled by the sign of Scorpio. And since the nature of Scorpio is secretive and mysterious, many things from this ancient culture are still hidden today.

THE MYSTERY OF HATHOR

I was awe-struck when I first saw the sculptured head figures representing Hathor at the Hathor Temple in Dendera, Egypt, and at the Temple of Isis, on the Isle of Philae in Egypt. I could not help but wonder if these were "alien" features, as I gazed at the small face, and the pointed ears which we have come to associate with the Vulcan, Mister Spock, of "Star Trek." I found this most curious. (SEE ILLUSTRATION SIX.)

Another thing that piqued my curiosity was the portrayal of Isis with wings. When I asked my tour guide about the possibility that Isis could have been an angel or archangel, he agreed that it was possible. Tom Kenyon, co-author of *The Hathor Material*, divulged, during a conference which I attended, that the inter-dimensional beings called Hathors were originally from Sirius. They beckon us to look further into symbols and meanings to find the truth. At times Isis was associated with Hathor or intermingled in reference; therefore, it is inevitable to study both Isis and Hathor to seek the true meaning.

Illustration Six: Hathor as seen on the columns at the Temple of Dendera and Isis

THE SIRIUS MYSTERY

The ancient Egyptians believed in visitors from Sirius, just as the Dogon tribe in Africa did.

One of the most interesting pieces of my research was to study these people of sub-Saharan Africa who are called the Dogon, and live in the present state of Mali. The nearest cities to them would be Timbuktu and Bandiagara.

The Dogons held a secret tradition of knowledge about the system of Sirius which would normally be impossible for a primitive tribe to know. There is evidence that they followed initiations connected to the tiny star, Digitaria (Sirius B) which orbits around Sirius. From their sand drawings, they demonstrate their knowledge of the details of the orbit of Digitaria and other astronomical information that did not become known to our western astronomy until the 1960's. However, the Dogons had knowledge of this for thousands of years.

Robert Temple, author of *The Sirius Mystery,* attributes a time that spaceships from the Sirius system landed in Sumeria. Zechariah Sitchin, who wrote *The 12th Planet*, gives a similar date for extraterrestrial activity in Sumeria, the difference being that they came from Marduk, a secret planet in our solar system. The upshot to this whole scenerio is that the aliens were viewed as gods by the primitive natives, and their appearance resulted in a considerable advancement in the Sumerian civilization.

In the book, *The Sirius Mystery*, Robert Temple demonstrates that the Dogon civilization had contact from visitors of a planet in the system of Sirius going back to 3000 B. C. The traditions of the Dogons are based in the ancient cultures of Sumer and Egypt. This whole concept is mind-boggling, except when you study the true ancient history of Egypt.

I had run across this piece of information by accident. The Dogons use the word "binu" to mean "returned," and falls under their custom of the totem, much like the Native Americans' totem. Members of a geneological family are grouped under the same totem. And to the Dogons, the totem means a clan, a name and a story. Their binu is associated with the human body, which has a mystical connection with a star in space. The Dogons believe in sacrifice for the purification of the universe. The steps of sacrifice are connected to the formation of a star and a totem of a person, animal or plant. Upon death, the victim is resurrected in the form of an adult human being. God gives the resurrected being an assignment associated with watching over the Universe. It was fascinating to learn how this binu was similar to the Egyptian Benu myth of rebirth.

Another captivating aspect of the Dogon culture was the "sirigi" mask design. Upon looking at ILLUSTRATION SEVEN, you will see that these two sample designs look like obelisks or rockets. Which one do you think they are? To the Dogons, these symbols represented the descent and impact of a spaceship which came to earth from Venus. The design is supposed to literally mean to them a "house with stories." The cosmic symbol of the resurrection is the "star of the tenth moon." The legend goes that this star will be perfectly formed when the spaceship of the Nommos, "the Monitors" of the universe, returns from the heavens.

Why do you suppose there are such connections between the Dogons and the Egyptians? It certainly is a cause for study to investigate the question often asked: Was Earth visited by beings from Sirius? We see connections of patterns between symbols in the culture of the Dogons and the Egyptians, making it a case to ponder.

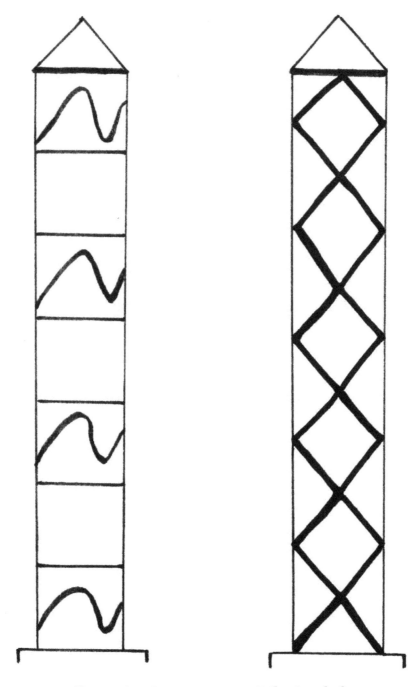

Illustration Seven: Dogon Tribe Symbols

THE SEVEN WONDERS OF THE WORLD

Of all the Seven Wonders of the Ancient World, only one remains intact--the Great Pyramid at Giza, Egypt. And when we study how old it may actually be, it becomes more of a mystery.

The Seven Wonders of the Ancient World were:

1. The Great Pyramid of Giza, which will be discussed below in more detail.
2. The Hanging Gardens of Babylon. Babylon was a city in ancient Mesopotamia, located on the Euphrates River, 55 miles south of Bagdad, Iraq. After the death of Alexander the Great, Babylon entered into its decline, as did the Hanging Gardens, now gone.
3. The Statue of Zeus. It was located at Olympia, Greece. This statue stood in the Temple of Zeus, giving tribute to the god of thunderbolts. It was destroyed by an earthquake in the Sixth Century A. D. The broken columns of this celebrated site were excavated in the 19th Century by Ernst Curtius, a pioneering archeologist with the German Archaeological Institute. About 438 B. C., a famous sculptor, Pheidias, was commissioned to create a statue of the most important of the gods of Greece. This statue was to serve as a shrine at the Olympics (or the Olympiads, as they were then called). The Olympics were celebrated every fourth year at the full moon. This entailed a week of religious festivity, with games of racing, jumping, and disc throwing, wrestling and boxing in a stadium positioned beside a sacred site of the gods.
4. The Temple of Artemis (Diana). This temple was located at Ephesus, an ancient Greece city on the west coast of Asia Minor. It was destroyed by the Goths in 262 A. D.
5. The Mausoleum at Halicarnassus. Halicarnassus was an ancient city on the north shore of the Ceramic Gulf in Caria. It is now the town of Bodrum in southwestern Turkey. The Mausoleum was built by the sister and the wife of the famous ruler, Mausolus, about 362 B. C. to 353 B. C. Only the ruins remain of this great mausoleum.

6. The Colossus at Rhodes. This was a gigantic, bronze statue of Helios, the Greek sun god, who stood overlooking the island of Rhodes. The statue was over 105 feet tall. It was destroyed in an earthquake in 223 B. C.
7. The Pharos Lighthouse of Alexandria. The Egyptians also called this the "Great Lighthouse" which was a revered lighthouse overlooking the Mediterranean Sea. Sostratos, a contemporary of Euclid, the Greek geometer, (300 B.C.) was the architect of the lighthouse. The white marble tower was over 330 feet high, on the eastern side of the island of Pharos, the name of the island on which it stood. The top of the tower was decorated with statues around which resinous wood burned constantly, thereby giving off a bright light. Its system of metal reflecting mirrors made the light a concentrated focus, visible over a massive distance. The site was destroyed in 1375 by an earthquake. Burji Mameluk Sultan Qaitby had ordered a fortress to be built around its foundations, which is all that remains of it in the bay off the coast of Alexandria. The function of the Pharos Lighthouse was to shine its beacon for ships that sailed at night, making it easier to see the entrance into its harbor, and to warn the sailors of the extremely shallow waters of the reef. Cleopatra's palace was located on Pharos Island.

THE MYSTERY OF THE GREAT PYRAMID OF GIZA

"In that day shall there be an altar to the Lord in the land of Egypt, and a pillar at the border thereof to the Lord. And it shall be for a sign and for a witness unto the Lord." -- Isaiah 19: 19-20

The above passage has been interpreted to refer to the Great Pyramid.

The magnificence of the Great Pyramid is overwhelming, as it stands three miles southwest of Cairo on the bank of the Nile. It has a ground area of 13.1 acres. The building is composed of at least 2.3 million limestone blocks, weighing approximately two and a half tons each. It has always remained a mystery how the feat of building this monument could have been accomplished by slaves at a time when there were no advanced architectural methods, as would have been required for this kind of plan.

The accuracy of the alignments of the Giza Pyramids to true north, south, east and west, could not have been accomplished by any science but astronomy. Who but master astronomers could have surveyed 13.1 acres and six million tons of mass? The development of modern star-mapping computer programs made it possible to simulate the ground as well as the sky of Giza over the last 20,000 years. Thus, a method was provided through which we could recreate the total vicinity of the Giza plateau. This confirms that old truths become stronger when they are translated into computer technology.

Researcher John Taylor devoted 30 years to collecting data on the Great Pyramid.

He discovered that if he divided the perimeter of the Great Pyramid by twice its height, it produced the quotient of 3.144, remarkably close to the value of PI, which is computed as 3.14159+. Consequently, the height of the Great Pyramid appeared to be in relation to the perimeter of its base, as the radius of a circle is to its circumference. This was too unusual to attribute to chance. Therefore, Taylor figured that the Great Pyramid was intended by its builders to incorporate the incommensurable value of PI. Moreover, this was a demonstration of the advanced knowledge of the builders of the pyramid. The PI was not correctly deduced to the fourth decimal point until the sixth century by the Hindu guru, Arya-Bhata. Taylor reasoned that the perimeter was intended to represent the circumference of the earth at the equator, and the height delineated the distance from the center of the earth to the pole.

Interestingly enough, Piazzi Smyth, who was a mathematician and son of the famous astronomer, Piazzi, had advocated the research of Taylor by presenting his conclusions in a paper to the Royal Society of Edinburgh in the 1860's. Because of this paper, Smyth received a gold medal for the accurate measurements of the Great Pyramid. To sum up his work, Smyth stated: "The Pyramid revealed a most surprisingly accurate knowledge of high astronomical and geographical physics…nearly 1500 years earlier than the extremely infantine beginning of such things among the ancient Greeks."

It was fascinating to follow the theory that the Great Pyramid was built as a technical scientific instrument and exact scale model of the Northern Hemisphere by an Egyptian culture further advanced than history can acknowledge. This theory suggests that the Great Pyramid contained the formula of the universe, and was destined to help humanity become orientated in the cosmos to apply finite measurements to time, space and the seasons of the yearly cycle.

It seems logical that the men of ancient wisdom may have found a way to store and preserve this special information, especially when we consider how the early scientists carefully guarded their knowledge by encoding it. Perhaps the answers to the Great Pyramid were to be revealed only to those who dared to make the effort to investigate. However, I feel that the answer to the Great Pyramid is soon to be revealed. During the Age of Aquarius, the hidden mysteries of the past will unfold, and science will move forward at an even swifter pace.

Some mystical facts: The Great Pyramid contains the King's Chamber which is exactly aligned with the Orion constellation belt. It was designed to mirror the constellation of Orion. In addition to this, I found out that the North Star is perfectly aligned to the descending passageway of the Great Pyramid. In ancient times, the North Star was called "Thuban," which meant a destiny of rebirth.

The Queen's Chamber, also within the Great Pyramid, is aligned perfectly to Sirius. At the temple of Isis at Philae, there is an inscription which says: "She, (the star of Isis), shines into her temple at New Year's day and she mingles her light with that of her husband, Osiris." The star of Isis was Sothis (Sirius, the Dog star).

It was so fascinating to confirm that the King's Chamber was associated with Osiris, while the Queen's Chamber was associated with Isis. Joseph Campbell wrote that when one has ventured down into the lower levels of the Great Pyramid, such as the Pit, the person is either on one side or the other. However, when an individual gets to the top, the points all come together and the Eye of God opens.

The three pyramids at Giza are a terrestrial map of Orion, giving us a perfect example of "As above, so below," a famous quote by Hermes Trismegistus, as he was called by the Greeks. This was an occult law formulated by Hermes, or Thoth as he was called by the Egyptians. Some sources say that Thoth was a god of creation, while others considered him a World Teacher who taught people the doctrine of "the Hidden Light." The pages of history tell us that the Great Pyramid was built around the Fourth Dynasty of Khufu (or Cheops, which was the Greek name for him) during the fourth millennium, B. C., but other evidence challenges this so-called history.

Thoth's quote, "As above, so below" has often been expressed as humanity's connection to the Universal Consciousness. Thus, "As above, so below" applies to the constitution of the universe with humanity, and has been adopted by the Rosicrucians, students of the Kabbalah, alchemists and Masonry. The rites of Masonry descended from the Ancient Egyptian Mysteries. The wisdom of the Egyptian Mysteries was the glory of the ancient world, and was adopted by the secret schools of other lands, such as the secret Hindu teachings of the Vedas and Upanishads of India.

In Chinese tradition, the earth is seen as a square figure and the heavens as a round figure. Their sacred temple of the moon is heavenly and round. The union of the square with the figure of the circle represented earth and heaven, male and female, the divine source of all things. (I find it provocative that Leonardo Da Vinci uses the circle and a square for the background of his drawing of the famous "Vitruvian Man.") For similar reasons, the square and the compass, instruments of those who made forms, became the symbols of Freemasonry. This led to the unique custom of tonsuring the heads of Roman Catholic monks, who shaved a circular area on the tops of their heads to symbolize the disk of the sun.

The inner history of Egypt with its pyramids and the Sphinx has been recognized to go back to the unrecorded days of the Divine Kings of the dynasties of Atlantis. These Divine gods or kings reigned for about 12,000 years before the Companions of Horus, who reigned for approximately 5,000 years. This is reported to have occurred before the first official First Dynasty of Mena, recorded about 3,000 B. C., based on Manetho's *History of Egypt*.

Concerning the time cycle just after the Great Flood, Egyptologists refer to an era called "Zep Tepi," which means "The First Times," when a preternatural group of gods appeared to empower the survivors. From Thoth and Osiris in Egypt, to Quetzalcoatl and Viracocha in the Americas, traditional stories of assistance in planting crops and other innovations are attributed to these gods.

The following information would lead one to question the written history of the Sphinx, and consider that it must have been of great importance earlier in time. Graham Hancock found through his research that the Sphinx is much older than originally believed. In his book, *The Message of the Sphinx*, Hancock presents evidence, through the computer technology which I mentioned, that specific plans for the Sphinx and the Great Pyramid in Giza were laid out during the Age of Leo, which would be 10,500 B. C. and not later, as given by "history." (In Edgar Cayce reading #5748-6, he was asked the date of the beginning and ending of the construction of the Great Pyramid, and he answered, "10,490 to 10,390 before the Prince entered into Egypt." He was referring to the B. C. date of that period, and Jesus as the Prince of Peace.)

It is no accident that the Sphinx has been arranged to face due East of the Rising Sun. All Egyptian rites were designed to perpetuate the rising of the sun. This symbolizes creation and hope for new life every day.

During one of my yoga sessions, it suddenly dawned on me that the position of the Sphinx was a yoga position. This realization led me into the discovery of an ancient term for energy called "Ga-llama." It is believed that this term originated with the ancient Egyptians going back to at least 142,000 years ago. Ga-llama is the basis of a system of Yoga known as Egyptian Yoga which is a technique for increasing energy and health through certain breathing exercises. Sometimes the breathing exercises are combined with basic ancient physical positions which we would consider as "yoga." To say that this discovery was fascinating is an understatement.

There is a temple in front of the Sphinx which has two sanctuaries. One is aligned to the east and one is aligned to the west. This has to do with the spring and autumn equinox alignment, and is associated with the solar cults of Egypt. This temple contains twelve statue positions, representing twelve hours of the day, twelve hours of the night, and the twelve months associated with the cycle of the Sun. There is some speculation that this could also represent the twelve rays of the sun, or solar rays to the earth, which more recently have gained entrance into modern knowledge through the Ascended Master Teachings.

Some sources say that the Sphinx symbolized the strength and spirit of the pharaoh, and that it was built to guard the Great Pyramid. It was considered a peaceful entity, except when the king was threatened by enemies. It was also considered an embodiment of the Sun God, giving it a title of "Horus of the Horizon." The Great Sphinx at Giza is 240 feet in length. Other sphinxes stand guard over the temples of Egypt. A row of sphinxes line the avenue between Luxor and Karnak, and sphinxes guard the remains of the Serapeum at Alexandria and the underground library.

According to Greek legend, the Sphinx was a creature with a female head and bird-like body. The gods sent it to Thebes, an ancient city of Greece, to punish the people. This creature was poised to eat anyone who was not able to answer this riddle: "Which animal has at first four legs, then two legs, then three legs?" No one could solve this riddle until Oedipus figured out that it must be a human. He stated that a human being crawls on all fours as a baby, walks on two legs as an adult, and walks with a stick in old age. When the Sphinx heard Oedipus answer thus, she plunged to her death on the nearby jagged rocks.

The ancient brotherhood who designed the Great Pyramid was aware of the constellation of Orion and its position in the sky, which perfectly aligned with the southern shaft of the King's

Chamber. This is why it was used in ancient initiations. The lowest point in the precessional cycle of Orion's belt occurred in 10,500 B. C. It was proven by computer calculations that the three stars in Orion exactly matched the layout of the three pyramids of Giza. Also, the Orion nebula is the nearest major site to earth of any massive star formation.

When we consider that the name *Orion,* is an ancient name meaning *the three kings,* we can understand how this referred to the three stars in Orion's belt, as well and the three pyramids of Giza. The three kings symbolize the three Divine aspects of Power, Wisdom and Love, which are the three main rays of the seven rays that emanate to Earth from the heavenly hierarchical system. This helps to explain the spiritual meaning of Orion as representing *the breaking forth of light.*

The physical Three Kings, also known as the Three Wise Men, spent a great deal of time studying records of ancient wisdom in Egypt, according to the Edgar Cayce readings. From these records of study, the Three Wise Men learned about the coming of the Messiah, and the special preparations by a Jewish sect called the Essenes. (Edgar Cayce reading #1010-17).

Graham Hancock explains how the dualism of the alignment of the heavens to the ground provides a clue to a physical entrance into a mythical place which serves as a connection between the earth and the sky. Is this one of the secrets that the ancients knew? There is more about this in Chapter Eighteen about the Duat.

We have discussed this heaven-to-earth connection through Orion and Sirius. *The Hathor Material* describes Sirius as a portal from other dimensions of the universe. The Sirius portal leads to a point in space/time where dimensional strands meet with non-physical dimensions. The Hathors, as channeled in *The Hathor Material,* said that they made contact with early Egyptians around 10,000 B.C. It was through the cult of the goddess Hathor that they were able to help the Egyptians achieve the Golden Age, which produced the Mystery schools. Through their metaphysical teachings, they were able to influence China, India and Tibet, as well as Egypt.

This is one reason why the Egyptian, Hebrew, Chinese, Hindu and Tibetan languages became "Sacred" languages, because of the sound vibration they produced. When these languages are put to music, the sound becomes even more powerful. The Hathors taught that sound is the principal vibration on earth which can go beyond physical sound, and is a natural vibratory reality. This allows one to move out of physical matter into a higher vibratory energy.

The teachings of the Brotherhood of Light speak about the entrance of a new root race that will bring in a new, higher dimension and consciousness to humanity. Cayce gave various references to a hall of records. In Edgar Cayce reading #5748-6, he refers to the Sphinx, "...there is a chamber or passage from the right forepaw to this entrance of the record chamber, or record tomb. This may not be entered without an understanding, for those that were left as guards may NOT be passed until after a period of their regeneration in the Mount, or the fifth root race begins." Also, in Edgar Cayce reading #519-1, he spoke about his client during a life reading, "The entity was among those that aided in the actual building of some of these buildings that still remain, and in the preparation of that one yet to be uncovered—the hall of records—where much may be brought to light."

Graham Hancock said that nothing is really new in the world, that we are constantly rediscovering the past. When we study the knowledge that lies in the annals of the past, we will find new answers to the dilemmas of modern times. We are on the brink of discovering the secrets of the past.

After my travels in the Egyptian temples along the Nile River, I was intrigued when I found that astrology was such a large part of their religion and mythology. Astrological symbols are predominantly on the ceilings of the temples. Myths that have been created in every culture have always had some thread of truth running through them.

Myths are based on actual happenings, but are altered as they get handed down through time. Perhaps this is why I found conflicting information on some of the gods and goddesses.

For instance, as I've mentioned, the sun god Re is also called Ra or Rah. And Hathor had more than one aspect. At first, many of these details were confusing and difficult to sort out, and that is an understatement. Nevertheless, I felt an excitement about being on the brink of discovering the secrets of the past.

CHAPTER FIVE

THE CALENDAR

The earliest Roman calendar had only ten months. All agricultural activity came to a standstill with the reaping and storing season at the end of the year. As a result, January and February were not included in the calendar. The crop activity did not resume until March, when the preparation and planting of the new crop season began. It is believed that this is why the zodiac begins in March under the sign of Aries.

After that, the Romans went to a lunar calendar, until Julius Caesar renovated the calendar with Sosigenes, a Greek astronomer. This turned out to make 46 B. C. an immense year of 445 days. Eventually, they adopted a solar year, modeled after the Egyptian calendar. The new Julian calendar began on January 1, 45 B. C., which was based on 365 days, with a leap year every four years.

The mid-eastern Egyptian zodiac had a slightly different time frame for the months. Their months varied widely from our Western months and our zodiac, as you will see. The Egyptian calendar was divided into twelve 30-day months, each containing three 10-day weeks, giving a total of 360 days. Five days were used to celebrate the birthdays of the gods and to await the rising of the star Sirius, called Sothis. These five days were called "epagomenal," meaning the days inserted between the last month of the old year, and the first month of the New Year to form a year of 365 days. On these five days they celebrated the birthdays of the gods of the Osiris cycle: Osiris, Isis, Horus, Set and Nephthys.

The Egyptians are credited with inventing the twenty-four hour day. They split it into twelve hours for daytime and twelve hours for nighttime. As you can see, twelve was a significant, recurring number.

The rising of Sirius signaled the flooding of the Nile River and the beginning of the Egyptian New Year in July. Each year, from July to October, the Nile spilled over its river banks, leaving a layer of silt. This event transformed the desert into temporary fertile land where their crops could flourish.

The New Year celebration was a time of merriment and music. The procession started at Edfu, at the Temple of Horus, and proceeded to Dendera, the Temple of Hathor, goddess of music, sound and love. What I found out about Hathor, was so intriguing, and will be expanded upon.

As I mentioned previously, the Egyptians were given the teachings of the Brotherhood of Light through Serapis Bey. And since there are two conflicting versions about Serapis, I present both of them for your clear understanding.

THE TWO VERSIONS OF SERAPIS

The First Version:

A source of confusion was the name Serapis. From the Ascended Master Teachings of the Brotherhood of Light, it gives the history of the Temple of Luxor as being founded by Serapis Bey. One version says that Serapis was an ancient king of the Egyptians who provided them with the foundation of their philosophical and scientific knowledge. In ancient times, this temple of Luxor was much different than it is today.

Serapis Bey was a priest in the Ascension Temple in Atlantis. He was assigned the special task of taking the sacred Ascension Flame, along with other members of the Brotherhood of Light, to a safe place in Egypt. He established a temple near the Nile River at Luxor. This became the

Luxor Temple for the Ascension Flame, and he has been a guardian for the flame since then. Serapis Bey is an Ascended Master, and serves the Spiritual Hierarchy of the Brotherhood of Light on the Fourth Ray.

I found it interesting that Serapis Bey had an incarnation as Amenophis IV, also known as Akhenaten, who built the temples at Thebes and Karnak. He made an attempt to focus on the worship of one god, but failed because of the strong, evil influence of the black priesthood at that time.

In Luxor, Egypt, you will find the Ascension Temple as a large square stone building, with a huge wall surrounding it. Inside is a large, beautiful courtyard. The Ascension Flame was taken to this place by Serapis Bey before the sinking of Atlantis. He established a temple around this area. Even though a retreat was built underground during the decline of Egypt, one of these ancient buildings had been retained above ground. The Entrance to the Ascension Retreat was reached through the ancient white building. The Ascended Master Teachings speak of buildings which are used by the Brotherhood of Luxor that are on an etheric level, the next highest dimension from the earth level.

The Ascension Temple was built in a square, composed of white, tall columns, twelve on each side. The secondary temples built within it, represented the activity of the Seven Rays that radiate from heaven to earth. The outer square room of blue represented the first ray of power. The next inner square room of yellow represented the second ray of wisdom. Then within that room was a pink square, which represented love and the third ray. The next inner room was a white square representing purity and the fourth ray. Following that was a green room representing healing and the fifth ray. The next inner room was rose-gold for the sixth ray representing peace. And the next inner room was violet which represented the seventh ray of transmutation. Each room was formed by large columns. The Flame Room, the center room, was completely white and crystalline. The outer temple was able to accommodate a large number of people. An initiate of the Brotherhood, began his training by seeing only the outermost activity of the blue ray until his consciousness was able to discern the higher vibratory action of the next higher ray.

The altar of the Flame Room was pyramid-shaped, with an Egyptian urn that held the precious Ascension Flame. The twelve virtues of the Godhead were represented around this altar as well as the twelve astrological signs. The Brotherhood of Luxor demanded complete obedience, and in return, they gave spiritual training in the control of vibration and energy, as well as the mastery of material substance.

The Second Version:

The Ptolemaic influence of the combination of Greek and Egyptian elements portrayed the god, Serapis, as Apis, the bull god, in a successful attempt to bring together the Greek and Egyptian worship of that era. This had a definite connection for the purpose of those times—bringing Egypt and Greece into religious unity with the belief in a common god. They saw him as the fertility god. Needless to say, this was a different version of the highly spiritual Serapis Bey, but it served a purpose.

The Greeks and the Egyptians who lived together in Alexandria believed that it was possible that the gods of one religion could be their gods of other names. Therefore, Ptolemy Soter decided to give form to the already existing Egyptian gods. He mixed Osiris, who would be Dionysus to the Greeks, with apis the bull god; and the result became Serapis the new god for Alexandria. Serapis upheld the Egyptian ideals, bearing the features of Zeus, the highest Greek god with Greek attire. Serapis was instantly popular with the Serapis cult which spread far across the Mediterranean area. The Temple of Serapis (the Serapeum) was located upon the citadel of Rhakatis. Today the remains are seen at the site of Pompey's Pillar in Alexandria. The Pillar of Pompey is where Caesar came to protest the killing of Pompey, the Roman general who was a member of the first triumvirate.

Underground, beneath the foot of the Serapeum, the more ancient remains of the Serapis temple can be seen as two long galleries cut out of natural rock and faced with limestone. One gallery contains curious niches in the walls where it is said that papyrus rolls were stored and part of the temple library. The other gallery leads to a sanctuary intended for the worship of Serapis.

Are you ready now for a different look at the Zodiac and its meanings, symbols and timing? The Egyptians have a treat in store for you. Let your imagination roam freely as you read through the Egyptian Mythology of the gods and goddesses. Allow the deities to speak to you. Each one has something to tell you. You might find that a particular god will capture your attention. The Egyptian culture is like that. It speaks to each person in an individual way. Have fun with finding your deity in the Zodiac.

CHAPTER SIX

After reviewing the pictures and journal of my travels in Egypt, I saw the need to continue researching the mystical Egyptian zodiac. I had accumulated a large volume of information. However, it needed to be sorted into some kind of order. It was like the myth of gathering the pieces of Osiris that were scattered all over Egypt. As a result, I decided to go into meditation periods. Then, after much of this meditation, research, contemplation and inspiration, here was how I was given the order of the Egyptian zodiac.

THE EGYPTIAN ZODIAC

The Zodiac is considered as one of the oldest universal forms of language with its unique symbols. We begin with the sign of Aries, which is the logical start of any study of the Zodiac as all parts of life start with spring and new life. And not surprisingly, the glyph for Aries represents the early sprouting of the plants of spring as they burst from the earth. Aries has also been compared to the "V" letter for victory. Let us now take a closer look at the Egyptian gods as we venture through the Zodiac.

ARIES

"I am Khnum, the shaper of humanity and controller of the waters of the Nile."

We begin with the Egyptian month of Pharmuthi, which runs from March 27 to April 25. This would be the approximate span of the Sign of Aries, and here it is represented as the Egyptian god, Khnum. Khnum was the lord of creation. He is depicted with the head of a ram and a human body. (SEE ILLUSTRATION EIGHT) Khnum holds the "was" in his left hand. The "was" is a scepter that combines the ankh, the symbol of life, with the "djed," the pillar of stability. While other gods, like Ptah, are depicted with just the "was," Khnum is shown with the "was" in the left hand and the ankh in his right hand.

According to the theology at Esna, Egypt, Khnum modeled the human body with clay on his potter's wheel. The potter's wheel is a term sometimes used to describe a person's ability to express and create a variety of things. Khnum is considered the shaper of humanity upon the celestial potter's wheel. He was also known as controller of the Nile's water. The waters of the Nile River overflowed upon the land, making it fertile every summer. Khnum controlled the annual flood by opening the sluice gates in the caverns of the god, Hapi.

Illustration Eight: Khnum

Khnum was given homage on Elephantine Island, where his temple had been erected during the Ptolemaic era, in the Fourth century B. C. Here the creation of the world was attributed to Khnum, who modeled the first man out of the mud of the Nile River.

Khnum had played a major role in harmonizing the myth of the divine origin of Queen Hatshepsut so that she could be the legal pharaoh from 1503 B. C. to 1483 B. C.

For twenty years she ruled, keeping her half-brother, Thutmosis III, in the background, while building the temple of Deir el Bahari on the west bank of the Nile at Thebes. After her death, Thutmosis III had her name removed from all the monuments, especially the mortuary temple at Deir el Bahari. In a series of reliefs at that temple, Amun is shown to visit Hatshepsut's mother, Queen Ahmose, and the queen conceives.

Khnum, is shown creating the royal infant and its "ka" on the potter's wheel (ILLUSTRATION NINE). The ka is portrayed as a second person, an exact replica of the young royal son, representing that both were created by Khnum simultaneously. The child is born, presented to Amun, and launched into its royal career. Thus, the ka is the etheric double which is the exact replica of the physical body, but of a finer substance (sometimes called the shadow). Also in this illustration, you will notice the tail with Khnum, which appears in the drawings of gods or pharaohs. Some sources call this a lion's tail. We also see the tail with Amon-Rah, Horus and Thoth. This tail came to be called the "shedshed" which the pharaoh wore attached to the waist belt, and was associated with rebirth, the means by which the soul mounted to heaven.

Illustration Nine: Khnum creating the child prince on the potter's wheel

In the rites of the ancient Egyptian Mysteries, which were applied mainly to the pharaoh, the king, we find the name of a celebration called "Sed." Sed means Feast of the Queue. During this jubilee, the pharaoh wore a false queue, attached to the waist in the belt that all pharaohs wore. This was considered a remnant of the skin-cradle, which was called the "shedshed." It was also was a symbol of the vehicle of the transportation of the soul into heaven. The shedshed's purpose was to signify that the initiate had passed through the sacrificial rites of initiation. (This is similar to the Dogon tribe's "binu" ritual).

Khnum's wife, Neith, was a warrior-goddess who carried arrows, and her symbol was a shield with two crossed arrows. (SEE ILLUSTRATION TEN.) The Greeks associated Neith with Athena, the goddess of hunting.

Maarten Raven, curator of the Egyptian collection in the Netherlands' National Museum of Antiquities, uncovered the tomb of a high priest at the temple of Aten in Memphis, Egypt, in 2002 A.D. The name of the high priest was Meryneith. An inscription found in his tomb said, "Meryneith, beloved of the goddess Neith." Included were symbols that had two hunting bows with the tips crossed at each end, describing the goddess, Neith. Since Akhenaten formed a new religion based on Aten, the sun disk, this places Meryneith in the time during the reign of Akhenaten, about 1347 B. C.

It must be stated here that Memphis had always been a vital urban and religious center, much like the American city of New York, which was once the capital of the United States. And, like Memphis, the capital was moved, but New York City always remained a significant area.

Illustration Ten: Neith

I almost let out a loud "Wow!" in the library, when I read that Plato wrote about a person who had seen the records of Atlantis at the temple of Neith in Sais, Egypt. Back in the Sixth Century B. C., Sais was the capital of Egypt. During this time, Solon, a Greek statesman, traveled to Sais, where he gathered information on Atlantis from their priests, and it was used in Plato's books, *Critias* and *Timaeus*. Today Sais is a little village located in the western part of the Nile Delta.

The goddess Neith wore a crown of red, and could appear as the Cow of the Heavens, a manifestation of Hathor, connected to the constellation of Sirius. Sobek is recorded as the son of Neith. He is the crocodile god who represented the power of the pharaoh, due to the strength and speed of the crocodile. A most curious temple at Kom Ombo is known for its double sanctuary dedicated to two gods: Haroeris (Horus the Elder) and Sobek the crocodile-god. There is a collection of crocodile mummies that are stored in a small chapel in honor of Sobek.

This period is compared to our Western version of Aries, the Ram. This is the time of year to take advantage of the key qualities of Aries, which include initiative, activity and leadership. It is your time to press for what you really want, to connect with the blossoming of nature and the momentum of vitality to move out into the world and celebrate the challenges of the spring of life. This is the moment to focus on what is important to you and your fulfillment, not forgetting that great pioneering ability that is there for any new project. Now is the time to take risks to elevate yourself, and act with daring and conviction. Bursting with enthusiasm, the Aries energy creates new ideas. Look for new opportunities to meet people and get into interesting new projects. This is a period of sowing seeds to produce what you want in the following months. Have faith in yourself and the dynamic, generous spirit of Aries. And remember to have fun with that wonderful Aries sense of humor.

CHAPTER SEVEN

TAURUS

*"I am Ptah-Seker-Ausar within the hidden place, great god,
lord of Ta-sert."*

The Egyptian month of Pachons runs from April 26 to May 25. Here we have the reign of the god, Ptah, who is known as the creator of form, or the creator of gods. Some sources claim that Ptah was the son of Nun and Naunet, who were spirits of the primordial ocean.

In the theory of creation found in countries such as Egypt, Phoenicia, Greece, the Polynesian Islands and Finland, the universe came into being from a Cosmic Egg. In the version found at Memphis, Egypt, Ptah, broke open an egg from which the sun and moon came into being. This brings the invisible fire of Tum, the heavenly fire which fell into earth, and in the mystery of Memphis takes the name of Ptah. This was a metaphysical fire manifested by the principles of the magical, mysterious Heliopolis, once a center of initiation at a temple that was eventually destroyed.

The word, Ptah, means "developer," or one who manifests, makes things. He was a craftsman. His duty was to protect goldsmiths and inventors. This cosmic architect, blacksmith and sculptor formed the word of the sun god Rah into a tangible spoken truth. Truth and justice manifest as a genuine route to realizing beauty here. Ptah's scepter is decorated with symbols of refinement and culture. He is most often depicted as a mummy with a close-fitting white cap (ILLUSTRATION ELEVEN). His wife was the lioness Sekhmet, and their son was the solar child and lotus-god Nefertum.

The Egyptians believed that Ptah raised the land of Egypt from beneath floodwaters by building dikes where the Nile River rose. Considered as coming from a Faraway land, Ptah established mountains and foreign lands, as well as Egypt. As a great, so-called olden god, Ptah came to Egypt by boat from the South in the horned headdress of Upper Egypt (which was south, geographically). In some reference books, Ptah is considered the father of Rah.

Ptah was often referred to as the maker of substance and a local creator god in Memphis. He gained popularity, as the city of Memphis did, and he became known as the ultimate source of all things.

Illustration Eleven: Ptah

To the Egyptians, the period from April 26 to May 25 came under the sign of Taurus, which loves beauty. To the Egyptians, Taurus was the Bull of Light, the reincarnation of Ptah as Apis, the Bull. In fact, the glyph for Taurus represents the head of a bull and/or a vase adorned with the horns of a bull. The vase endows receptive and productive abilities, and the horns symbolize vigor in challenging situations.

The Seven Pleiades in Taurus have been called the Seven Stars of the Christian Book of Revelation. In this celestial region, we also find the esoteric Perseus, the solar Hercules, symbolizing the Higher Self who tames the beast-nature and rescues Andromeda, the Morning Star.

If we consult the Ascended Master Teachings, such as in *Law of Life* by A. D. K. Luk, we have a symbol of power and might with Hercules, instead of Taurus the Bull charging into the scene. Hercules, the Elohim of Power, is the first of the Seven Elohim whose activity is to carry out God's Will. The Seven Elohim are the creative builders of the Earth. Hercules, from Greek mythology, represents the struggling soul who goes through life's tests and failures to achievement and success. Hercules empowers the positive qualities of earth. He gives the vision of overcoming, rising above the negative, a hint of the glory awaiting us when we are victorious over the obstacles of life.

This cycle is sacred to stability and power. This is the time of year to get back to the basics of life. Get grounded, come down to earth in a practical way. The image is the farmer plowing the earth, regenerating the soil for new growth. The energy of Taurus is slow, steady progress. The keywords for Taurus are persistence, endurance, and sensuality, with the influence of Venus for love, beauty and heightened sensual touch. Use the resources of money, talents, and physical abilities to manifest functional things that will be permanent and enduring. The patient Taurean never gives up. Look into financial and material matters to examine what may enhance your self worth. Make decisions carefully and deliberately, evaluating everything. Find ways to establish bonds with people who are important to you. Forget about feeling shy in any way. Let others see the good that lies deep within. Look for new opportunities in love. The energies of Taurus bring physical beauty, strength and security.

CHAPTER EIGHT

GEMINI

"I am Horus, the great sky god, who shares his divinity with the pharaoh."

For this period we have the Egyptian month of Paoni, which runs from May 26 to June 24. This time period is the reign of Horus, god of the sky and protector of the pharaoh. Born after the body of his father, Osiris, was mummified by Anubis, the protector of tombs, Horus became a divinity with dual characteristics. The glyph for Gemini looks like the Roman numeral "II" for the number two. This symbol expresses duality between the subconscious and conscious mind--or masculinity and feminity--in the exchange between two subjects or objects, as it generates creative movement.

It was common for Egyptian gods to have various names. Re-Harakhty was "Horus of the Horizon," and Harsiesis was "Horus, Son of Isis." The special cult centers of Horus were Behdet, Hierakonoplis, and Edfu.

When visiting the Temple of Horus at Edfu, Egypt, the traveler will see two statues of Horus: one at the outer entrance and one at the inner entrance. He is called both the Heavenly Horus and the Earthly Horus, signifying the Divine body and the Earth body working together as one. This can also be regarded as the Elder Horus (Haroeris) and the Young Horus (Harpocrates).

Horus was a powerful solar god with the falcon's head adorned by a double crown. He is also portrayed as a winged sun-disk.

As a sky god, with the head of a falcon, Horus soars high above the Earth on the wind. The falcon here is a symbol of the higher mind. Agile and observant, Horus shows us the importance of rising to the demands or challenges of the moment. He reveals secrets linked to the sun, which would always be present in a desert country such as Egypt. He brings survival skills and a flair for seeing the panorama of life. Horus is the son of Osiris and Isis, and his wife is Hathor.

The ancient Egyptians saw Horus in the period of Gemini as the god who had the sun and the moon as his two eyes. In a battle with Set, Horus had one of his two eyes torn out, but Horus was able to find it again. This was the Sacred Eye that is used in numerous inscriptions for amulets and to bestow good fortune. This is the Eye of Horus, considered to be the moon, and very powerful and protective.

Harpocrates, the younger aspect of Horus by Greco-Roman iconography, often has the wings of Eros on his back and the double Pharaonic crown (pschent). He is always depicted holding his index finger to his lips, a Roman characteristic gesture as a warning not to divulge the secrets of the Initiation into the Isiac mysteries.

Horus compares to the sign of Gemini, and the higher mind which is flexible enough to adjust to the changes thrown upon the person born under Gemini. According to the teachings of the Brotherhood of Light, it is the time period for the reign of the Cosmic Christ—the focus of Divine Love—the human Christ, the Son/Sun working through personality or ego. It is the Divine Image in the body of flesh.

The symbol of duality is depicted by the twins. In Greek mythology it was Castor and Pollux, the twin heroes whose heads glow together as one light. They also symbolize immortality: one is on the earth while the other is living in the heavens. There is no death, but a rebirth on a higher plane of existence. In the original Babylonian zodiac, Gemini is portrayed by male and female. In Egyptian mythology, the twins are Horus the Younger and Horus the Elder.

Horus is often shown with his wife, Hathor, depicted as the cow-horned goddess. Also, upon her forehead, she often has the Uraeus, the Egyptian Serpent, which is the protector of the Solar Disk of God Consciousness. Those who have the Uraeus in this spot of the forehead have passed the initiations given to pharaohs, and their wives.

Horus succeeded Osiris after Osiris went into the underworld, but not without a fight. When Osiris went into the underworld, the evil Set became the king. Horus challenged Set for kingship. The gods held a trial. Thoth and Shu voted for Horus. However, Rah voted for Set. Isis disguised herself as a beautiful young woman in order to persuade Set that he should not rob a son of the birthright. Nevertheless, Set and Horus had to settle the dispute in a contest. Each of the two men had to turn themselves into a hippopotamus and stay under water for three months. Horus castrated Set, turning him into a black pig. Then Set tore out Horus's eye and flung it beyond the horizon. This plunged the world into darkness. Thoth collected the fragments of the eye together, in which he created the full moon. He gave Horus the "Ougjat eye" (also called "Wadjet") which means "the Eye of Eternity," and it gave the power to conquer death. After the gods sent a letter to Osiris in the underworld, Osiris said that he would send demons to harass them if Horus did not win the throne. And so Horus became king, and Set was assigned a position in the sky where he became god of storms.

In ILLUSTRATION TWELVE, Horus is seen leading Hunefer to the weighing of the soul.

This drawing represents a sequence taken from the
papyrus of Hunefer in *The Book of the Dead*.

This is the time of year to develop a network of communications and personal contacts. The keywords for this Gemini time are versatility, ingenuity, and elocution, which, is the ability to speak well. It is a good time to expand friendships, business and community associations. Search out organizations or groups that have interests in common with you. Enjoy discovering new avenues of knowledge, and expressing this to other people. That is one of the qualities important to Gemini: sharing information. Geminis are always on the go, in an effort to satisfy that mental curiosity. Any endeavors of reading, writing, research, exploring areas of curiosity will stretch your ability to grow now. Find time to do the things you enjoy most, so that you can feel free from day-to-day routines and burst out into new areas of interest. Any mental work, such as using affirmations will work well to bring you what you desire and to stay focused. Gemini energy is very intuitive, so try to expand those skills that help you reach into higher levels of mind, such as meditation. You can also use this unique energy to recapture the world of wonder that keeps Geminis as youthful as the eternal child.

Illustration Twelve: Horus leading Hunefer to the weighing of the soul

CHAPTER NINE

CANCER

"I am Nephthys, mistress of the underworld."

The reign of Nephthys, the moon goddess, is from June 25 to July 24, the Egyptian month of Epep. Nephthys (Nebt-het, meaning "lady of the house" of Osiris) is sometimes shown as an attractive young woman with abundant baskets of fruits and flowers. (In ILLUSTRATION THIRTEEN, she is shown with a headpiece that to me, at first looked like a coffee grinder. Then through research I learned that it meant "lady of the house.")

The glyph for Cancer represents a fetus curled up within the uterus—an encounter between polar opposites—evolving to create a new form of life.

Nephthys is the sister of Isis, and joined Isis in caring for Osiris after he was killed by Set. This caused Nephthys to leave Set and join her sister in mourning. Sometimes the two mourning goddesses are portrayed as hawks in Egyptian art. It was the custom at Egyptian funerals for two women to represent Isis and Nephthys, often wearing hawk masks, to lament over the mummy of the departed.

Illustration Thirteen: Nephthys

Nephthys and Isis are special guardians, given the task of guarding the rays that radiate from the godhead, as the rays descend to earth. Nephthys portrays the magical power to realize that unseen forces can be more powerful than seen forces. This represents an ancient truth: That which appears to be real is not always real, or the test of appearances.

Nourishment, home and family are the special treasures of Nephthys. She plays the dual role of wife to the fierce god, Set, and mother of Anubis. Osiris was her brother and father to her son, Anubis.

Plutarch wrote in late Egyptian tradition that Anubis was the son of Osiris and Nephthys. The story goes that while Isis was busy searching for the body of Osiris, she learned that Nephthys had performed a magical ritual before the death of Osiris, to present herself to him as Isis. Through this sexual event, Nephthys conceived a son, Anubis. (Remember that Set was castrated by Horus.)

The barren marriage of Nephthys to Set can be compared to the stark desert wastelands, while the fertility with Osiris, the father of her child, suggests a life-giving oasis. Creativity on every level is stimulated during her cycle. The Egyptian New Year begins during this period on July 19, when the star, Sirius, rises near the Sun. On the day of the Egyptian New Year, the Sphinx, as a Lionized Human, comes to life in a resurrected form.

At the temple of Hathor in Dendera, Egypt, as well as at the temple of Esna, Cancer is the Scarab, the symbol of death and the resurrection of new life. Thus, the Egyptians depicted the scarab beetle as the constellation of Cancer. There has been much speculation as to why the sign of Cancer was given primary importance and shown in the center of the zodiac at Dendera, as I will explain later.

To the Chaldeans, the constellation of Cancer was a conduit through which the souls passed into the earthly life. And the teachings of Ancient Wisdom say that Cancer is "the Gate in." This means it is the entrance where the soul takes physical incarnation under Cancer as the ascendant, or rising sign, for a cycle of spiritual unfolding. When the soul is highly evolved, this placement of Cancer creates a firm foundation for the future. Then it can give a special type of nourishment to help others realize their soul's purpose. The opposite sign or higher octave of Cancer is the constellation of Capricorn. Capricorn was considered "the Gate Out," the road through which the soul returned to Osiris in the heavens.

To add more clarity to this concept, let us consider that there are only 4 days of special significance when the earth, moon and sun are in distinctive relation to each other. These distinctive positions are the Equinoxes and the Solstices. The Solstice of Cancer occurs on June 21, and the Solstice of Capricorn occurs on Dec. 21. The Solstice of Cancer and the Solstice of Capricorn are called the two Gates of heaven because of the powerful celestial energies that can bring balance and healing at this time.

Nephthys represents Cancer and the Moon Child. In the ancient teachings, this is where the Elohim Vista appears, who represents the All-seeing Eye of God which is seen at a special solar point at the Great Pyramid of Giza. Elohim Vista embodies the god-virtue of Concentration. Nothing can truly be accomplished—from the most spiritual to the mundane activities of life—without concentration. There can be no mastery of life unless there is concentration and determination to rise above the masses of mediocrity. Cancer's task is to develop one facet of living and excel in at least one talent and expression.

Therefore, at this time of the year, turn inward to nurture your personal and emotional power. The keywords for Cancer are sympathy, sensitivity and affection. Let your joy child have expression. You may find that feeling joyful and happy as a child opens your mind to creative imagination that can be nurtured even further when you couple it with meditation. Do you have anything that needs releasing or clearing from childhood? If so, now is the time to release baggage from the past. Home and family relationships are also strengthened during this time, which is important to fulfill your need to feel connected and secure. You may also feel the need to nurture significant others as spouse, parent, friend, caregiver, therapist, etc. If they need your help, and ask for it, now is your opportunity to share your time with those you love. Cancerians have a strong urge to protect their loved ones, no matter what. The Cancer energy may display some protective shell of shyness. This is not a weakness, but a withdrawing process in order to gather strength.

CHAPTER TEN

LEO

"I AM Sekhmet, daughter of Rah, fearless lioness and cat goddess."

An Egyptian myth says that the Sun was in Leo and that the moon was in Virgo when the universe was created. The Egyptian solar disc was shown as flanked by lions. The Sun in Leo, to the Egyptians, signaled flooding, so much so that the lions were represented on the irrigation gates of the Nile River. There have been many claims that the Sphinx is a composite of the symbol of Leo and Virgo.

The glyph for the sign of Leo is a symbol that represents both a majestic flame and the tail of a lion. This symbol suggests a fiery passion, as well as the expression of pride.

This is the period from July 25 to August 28, called the month of Mesore. It is represented by the goddess Sekhmet, sometimes called Tefnut. To describe her, let us go to the myth of the Lost Sun.

Sekhmet, the solar daughter of Rah, the Sun god, became angry with her father and left Egypt. Sekhmet means "the powerful one," having many manifestations and names in the temples of Egypt.

Since she was the Eye of the Sun god, the loss of the Sun created a serious problem. Therefore, it was necessary to persuade Sekhmet to return to Egypt. Her brother Shu, the god of light and air, and Thoth, the scribe, were sent to Nubia to bring her back.

Upon finding Sekhmet, Shu and Thoth used rattles made of faience (metal), called *sistra,* and other musical instruments to transform the irate Sekhmet into the tame, domestic cat goddess, Bastet. Thereafter, the sistrum and the *menit,* another rattling instrument, a collar of beads, became typical objects of Sekhmet.

Because of the worship and honor given to the cat goddess, Bastet, all cats in Egypt were considered sacred. House cats (called "miu") were often mummified when they died and were buried with their owners, as previously noted.

Sekhmet has been known as a fierce lioness and goddess of war (SEE ILLUSTRATION FOURTEEN). A brave defender, she preserved the human race through guarding the Sun god against an uprising. Sekhmet demonstrates what can be accomplished through principles such as courage and dignity. She is fiery, with a determined purpose. As the wife of Ptah, Sekhmet generates reverence, as well as fear.

Illustration Fourteen: Tefnut, an aspect of Sekhmet

While we are on the subject of lions, I was captivated with the following information. In 2001, French archaeologist, Alain Zivie, discovered a preserved lion skeleton in the ancient tomb of Maia, who was a wet nurse to Tutankhamun. Although inscriptions in Egypt account for the breeding and burial of lions, the fact that no lion remains have ever been found made this a significant find and addition to knowledge of ancient ritual. Tombs associated with Tutankhamun, such as Maia's tomb, were found in a burial ground south of Cairo, across the Nile River from the first capital of ancient Egypt, Memphis. The skeleton of the lion was found in an area of the tomb dedicated to Bastet. One theory was that the lion may have been considered an incarnation of the god, Mahes, the son of Bastet. The condition of the bones reveals that it lived to an old age and was kept in captivity. While the researchers are still puzzled over this lion mummy, one thing was certain: it was an important lion.

During this time of year, the crops are ripe and the earth is fertile. It is important to learn how to express yourself in an original way. The keywords for Leo are confidence, vitality and self-expression. Something is always special about a Leo. The Leo energy is warm, loving and generous with a flair for the dramatic as they play to an appreciative audience where they are in their element. The great sense of drama makes the great romantic. Take time to explore where your special talents lie, so that you can find pleasure and fulfillment, perhaps in one of the arts. Could there be a budding writer or artist inside you? Find methods to relax and enjoy yourself. Allow yourself to give birth to new ideas. Let your imagination run loose. Now is the time to get out and socialize, so that the world can experience your magnetic personality, enthusiasm and power. Let your inner beauty fulfill that desire to shine as you improve your self-esteem, public image or leadership abilities, so typical of Leo. You are in your glory when you are expressing affection to your mate or children. The Leo energy compensates for any failings with a sunny disposition, sense of fun and many social skills.

CHAPTER ELEVEN

VIRGO

"I am Isis, the divine mother."

From August 29 to September 28, we have the Egyptian month called Thoth. This is the reign of Isis, the archetype of the divine mother, represented as an angelic, madonna-like figure (SEE ILLUSTRATION FIFTEEN). In fact, the ancient model for the Madonna is Isis, with Horus at her breast. Virgo is an ancient symbol of purity and wholeness. The Egyptians considered Isis as a savior, the one who heals and restores Osiris, whose death at the hands of the evil Set, is avenged by her son Horus.

The glyph for Virgo is portrayed as an "M" that has a slash through the last leg. It is said to represent the body and wings of Virgo, with the extra stroke of the slash suggesting a seed-cluster and a pure type of character. The legs of the "M" are associated with the intestines, symbolizing analysis and selection.

Isis is considered the goddess of healing and magic because of her healing of Osiris, and others later on. She is portrayed as very clever, yet kind and nurturing. She created a sanctuary of the home, providing a shield from harsher realities. The strength of mercy, beauty and the magic of true love are all revealed by Isis.

Illustration Fifteen: Isis

After having left Horus at Butos, she fashioned a magical boat out of papyrus, and traveled the entire empire of Egypt. As she found the scattered parts of Osiris, she encased each one in a magical mummy composed of wax, grain seed and incense. Eventually, she recovered all of the parts of Osiris except the phallus, which had been thrown into the river and eaten by a fish. Isis was able to reproduce this organ in gold, and performed magical ceremonies to insure the life of Osiris in the underworld. Then she returned to Horus and saved him from the stings of scorpions.

The name of Isis means "throne," hinting at a very elevated position. Isis has the power to hold the thought of the throne of God within the individual mind. Thus, we often see the image of the throne upon the head of Isis in some Egyptian representations of her.

When Horus was born, Isis created special medications and nursed him in her tender way, which is often illustrated in art, associating her with the Virgin Mary and Jesus. (It was reported that Sigmund Freud kept a statute of the image of Isis with Horus suckling her breast in his office.) Isis knew how to use concoctions of herbs, berries, seeds and even the milk of the gazelle to heal the eye sockets of Horus when he lost his sight. She could even cure, through the oral power of invocation, without the use of potions. The name of Isis was believed to be a weapon against any harm or illness. After a person stayed a few days in the temple of Isis for a fee, they could expect a perfect healing. She became a personal savior through her empathy with people and grief over the death of Osiris. She did not live on some distant Mount Olympus, but among the people. Therefore, the rites of Isis became the most popular mystery religion which spread from Egypt to Greece and Rome.

The mysteries of Isis continued to have an effect on humanity. It contributed to the opera, *The Magic Flute*, by Mozart, in the eighteenth century, and Madame Blavatsky in the nineteenth century wrote the book, *Isis Unveiled*, an incredible esoteric work. The first edition of *Isis Unveiled* sold out in nine days. The crux of this work unfolded the concept of an eternal Essence, the Universal First Cause, of which the spirit of man is a part. It was said that this book was channeled from certain members of the Brotherhood of Light. Isis had been depicted with a veil over her head, which symbolized mystery.

The activities sacred to Isis were the flooding of the Nile River, which brought life-giving waters, along with the appearance of the star Sirius and the Egyptian New Year. The virtues of Isis were faithfulness and honesty. Thus, Isis became the divine symbol of a loyal wife.

This coincides with the god-virtues of service and purity of Virgo. In the sacred teachings of the Brotherhood of Light, Virgo is the goddess of Earth, the Cosmic Being who brought the pure white radiating substance of quartz to earth when all was in its original pristine state. She directs the substance of the planet and the Gnomes, the elemental beings of the Earth element. She raises and purifies the mineral elements of earth into light substance.

Virgo was also the Greek Woman with Wings, who descended from heaven to teach how to harvest earthly energies.

During this time, devote yourself to working more efficiently and productively. It is a good time to improve work relationships. The keywords for Virgo are efficiency, service and discernment. Find ways to apply ideas and methods to get the most out of everything. Be practical and organized, and don't take on more than you can handle. There may be a tendency to analyze the smallest of details, so be sure to try to see the big picture as well. Concentrate on improving your diet, exercise and health in general. You can help others best when you are in your healthiest form. You also have a healing touch at this time of year when you feel compassionate and sensitive to the needs of others. This is the harvest time of the year. Virgo reaps what has been sown in the spring. The Virgo energy is in touch with the earth energies, which give its bounty to those who are attuned and who try to help the earth and the need for conservation. There is a distaste here for anything stupid, vulgar or gross. There is an instinct to bring order out of confusion. Virgo knows that what he/she does to the earth will affect humanity.

CHAPTER TWELVE

LIBRA

"I am Anubis, claimer of hearts."

This period covers the Egyptian month of Paopi, from September 29 to October 27, which is the reign of Anubis. Referred to as "the claimer of hearts," Anubis has the head of a black jackal on a human body. Black signifies the color of the corpse after mummification, and Anubis is the god of embalming. This half-dog, half-human image often adorns burial or entombed artifacts, because he was honored as the supervisor for those about to make the important journey to the afterlife. His jackal head symbolized the scavengers who roamed grave sites, as well as his ability to communicate with the dead.

The glyph for Libra is made up of two superimposed dashes. The first dash symbolizes an interrupted equilibrium, and the second dash symbolizes the restoration of equilibrium.

Anubis helped Isis in her search for the scattered pieces of Osiris, and he watched over the body while Isis revived him. Anubis is the signpost of help to the soul who is having trouble finding its way back home to the afterlife. With his sixth sense, he can pick up the scent of the trail to return home. Thus, Anubis has the ability to travel between two worlds with an uncanny intuitive power.

As we see in ILLUSTRATION SIXTEEN, Anubis is performing the most important of rituals that all Egyptians must pass in order to enter the underworld (heaven). The scale has the Goddess of Truth on the center pole, and Anubis is testing the tongue of the balance. The feather represents the symbol of truth, and the heart of the deceased in the jar must counterbalance the feather. Anubis supervises the weighing of the soul, while Am-mit, the composite crocodile-lion-hippo body of the "Swallower of the Dead" anxiously awaits for the opportunity to eat the soul, in the event that the soul does not pass the test. (Am-mit appears in Illustration Eighteen.) If the feather and the heart weighed the same, it meant that the deceased had been good. He had earned the right to go to the Field of the Reeds, the beautiful realm where the gods lived forever. However, if the heart was heavier than the feather, it meant that the soul of the deceased did not deserve the Field of the Reeds, and that the Swallower of the Dead could eat the heart with its sharp teeth. This event was undesirable to the Egyptians, and so the art of mummification became necessary to keep the body from decaying. This process took forty days. First the organs were taken from the body. Then the body was put in a saline solution to dry out, followed by a coating of oil and wax. Finally the body was stuffed with sand and wrapped in linen strips. The major organs of the body were placed in funeral jars. The mummies were placed in tombs.

Illustration Sixteen: Anubis

Libra is the sign of scales and balance. Anubis is counterpart to Libra in the mystical teachings of Ancient Wisdom. Anubis brings matters into balance and justice, in order that the soul can achieve freedom from the entrapments of overindulgence. But of most importance was the weighing of the soul's heart. If the heart was too heavy (from depression or life's sorrows), then the soul could not get into the underworld (heaven).

One myth said that Anubis was the son of Rah, the god of the sun at noontime. Another version, by Plutarch, said that he was the son of Osiris and Nephthys. So here we have another conflict in sources.

In the Egyptian *Book of the Dead* papyrus of Hunefir, there is a sequence of pictures showing Anubis leading the deceased Hunefir and then weighing his heart on the scale. Then Thoth is recording the weight, and Horus is shown presenting Hunefir to Osiris on his throne. A prayer said by the deceased went like this: "Oh heart of my body…don't weigh heavy against me…for you are my ka, who is in my body." The meaning for "ka" here is "the spirit." In other references the "ka" is mentioned as the Overself, or as the soul.

In the language of the Egyptians, *The Book of the Dead* was called, "Pert Em Hru," which meant, "Emerging by Day." It was designed to be read out loud to the person who was dying, for the purpose of giving the subconscious mind control over the strange events that occur during the close of the physical cycle. *The Book of the Dead* contained magical spells, maps and prayers to help the soul get through the dangers of the underworld such as demons, snakes and lakes of fire. The spells helped the soul to reach the Hall of Judgment, wherein Osiris greeted it. Then the soul had to swear that his life had been good, leading to questions asked by Osiris. If the answers pleased the gods, then the final test came, which was the weighing of the heart.

This is the time of year to strengthen partnerships in love and in business. You can also play a role in keeping the family ties connected. The keywords for Libra are balance, diplomacy and relationships. Librans are diplomats and will turn on the charm and smiles to keep everything in harmony, above all else.

Libra is the "telephone" person who is so great at keeping everyone in touch. It is important to learn how to meet the needs of the significant others in your life, as well as your own needs for success, fairness and balance. It is a good time to put your affairs in order and bring harmony to all matters. You will gain the most by focusing on how you can help others for the good of everyone concerned, and how your social relationships can help professional objectives. During this time, you will sense how to balance your energies with another person. You will prefer to keep peace with your adaptable, pleasing manner, and not rock the boat. As you continue to work on self-awareness and inner adjustment, you become more self-reliant enabling you to stand up for your own beliefs, even when it may not be in agreement with others around you. The Libran energy loves activities that combine sociability and affection such as weddings, anniversaries, or any gatherings of family and friends. This is the great romantic that appreciates special gifts such as flowers that satisfies the soul's need for beauty.

CHAPTER THIRTEEN

SCORPIO

"I am Set, lord of the barren desert."

The Egyptian period for Scorpio is from October 28 to November 26, and the month is called Athor. This is the reign of Set. He is the god of evil. In some sources, I saw him referred to as Typhon, the dragon of ignorance and perversion.

The glyph for Scorpio is the letter "M" with the last leg becoming an arrow, representing the stinger of the scorpion, which can kill others or even the scorpion himself. This symbol is also seen as an expression of the mystery of redemption where death through the means of the stinger symbolizes renewal of life through water, resulting in rebirth.

Set was the lord of Upper Egypt, husband of Nephthys, and killer of Osiris. He invented the use of bows and arrows, and has evil red eyes. Although the pig was hated by the Egyptians, it was sacred to Set. This ferocious god wears a pig's head and has a scorpion tail. Could this be where the term "pig-headed" came into being? (SEE ILLUSTRATION SEVENTEEN.)

Illustration Seventeen: Set

The evil Set persuaded seventy-two people to join him in a conspiracy against Osiris. He designed a chest of attractive jewels to exactly fit the body of Osiris. After Osiris returned from a long journey, a feast was held. During the feast, Set made a spectacle of the chest, and promised that the one who could most easily fit inside it would own it. Each of the princes attending the feast took a turn in the box. But most of them were either too short or too tall. However, when Osiris put himself down in the chest, the seventy-two connivers immediately nailed it shut, and poured melted lead over every crack to seal it permanently. Then they carried the chest to the River Nile, casting it into the area where the Nile joined the sea. Reportedly, this happened on the seventeenth day of Athor. It was also said that this evil deed occurred in the 28th year of the reign of Osiris.

A great price was paid when Set thus killed his brother, Osiris. His wife left him, and he was no longer a part of the Great Company of Egyptian gods. In revenge of the death of his father, Horus battled Set for three days and three nights. As Horus was about to kill Set, Isis was overcome with compassion for her brother Set, and stopped his death. Isis found a way to restore the scattered parts of Osiris. Then Osiris became god of the underworld, which is the Egyptian heaven in the fourth dimension.

As lord of the desert, foreign countries, storms and confusion, Set begets order out of chaos. He helps us to learn how to overcome in the face of distinct evil. The Scorpion qualities of intense anger, passion, restlessness and material importance can be transcended when the character of Set learns to transmute to the soaring eagle.

I need to mention another god figure that has the symbol of the scorpion, and that is the scorpion goddess, Selkit. A scorpion sits on top of the head of Selkit. This symbol tells us that she had magical power against the insect's sting, and that she repelled evil. Selkit was a protector of the throne of the pharaoh.

Selkit was a guardian goddess of the pharaoh's sarcophagus. She adorns the sarcophagus of Har-em-hab stretching her protective wings on the south-west corner of the coffin. Har-em-hab was the pharaoh who reigned after Ay and Tutankhamun (1349-1319 B. C.). Selkit is also present with outstretched arms on the funeral shrine or chest containing the viscera of King Tutankhamun. (The visera were the heart, lungs, liver, stomach and intestines of the deceased.) Selkit was present during the embalming process, as she was responsible for these organs. She also prevented Apep, the serpent, from attacking the Sun God's ship in the underworld.

This knocked my socks off: From the book, *Maya/Atlantis, Queen Moo and the Egyptian Sphinx* by Augustus Le Plongeon, I learned that Selkit has her name rooted in Mayan origin!

I was captivated by the information which connected the Mayans and the Egyptians. In Mayan lore, Selkit is referred to as the goddess Selk, with title of "the great reptile" or "directress of the books." Her reign was given in the region of Amenti, called the Land of the West, or West Indies, where Selk was assigned the task of notching on the palm branch of Thoth the years of earthly life. This gives her a close association with Thoth. It is suggested that Selk or Selkit is connected to the islands in the West Indies called, "Zinaan," by the Mayans, meaning, "scorpion."

In Egypt, the death of Osiris was observed on the 17th day of Athor, the time of the autumn equinox. This was considered the time when the sun entered the six lowered signs of the zodiac. An ark was fashioned in the shape of the crescent moon. On the nineteenth of Athor, the priests announced that Osiris was found, and that his resurrection was on the third day of the moon.

Also, in Egypt there was an annual ceremony following the autumn equinox called "the Nativity of the Sun's Walking Stick." This ceremony was derived from the belief that the sun had become weak and impotent at this time of the year, therefore needing a walking stick to lean upon.

During this period of time, it is favorable to eliminate old habits or any behaviors that have held you back. The keywords for Scorpio are regeneration, secrecy and power. Take a hard look at power issues, fears, any emotional blocks or patterns from the past that may be impeding you. Do you need to be too much in control of others to the point of making them uncomfortable? Counseling, or past-life regression, may be helpful during this time. The Scorpio energy has the ability to dig deeper than most signs, and can uncover clues or facts that may have been hidden until now. This energy can manifest like Inspector Clouseau, who unconsciously stumbles into fresh discoveries, or the foxy Detective Columbo, who probes and persists until he has the object of his chase in his clutches. A Scorpio will persevere until the bitter end with a situation that needs enormous staying power. The Scorpio energy is also passionate and loyal, giving the ability to plunge into the depths of emotion to destroy what is no longer needed and make way for renewal and rebirth. The image of the phoenix bird rising out of the ashes symbolizes the magical ability of the Scorpian to be reborn, arising from the depths of the changing forces of nature into new heights of understanding and empowerment.

CHAPTER FOURTEEN

SAGITTARIUS

"I am Thoth (the moon) who brings Maat (true order) and heals the Sacred Eye."

From November 27 to December 26 is the month of Choeak.

The glyph for Sagittarius is an arrow which in this case represents speed, accuracy and confidence. This is an arrow that does not stray from its path, but travels directly to its target. The arrow transcends space and time with the ability to join earth with the heavens, just as the Sagittarius personality has a wide breadth of expansion.

This period is ruled by Thoth. ILLUSTRATION EIGHTEEN shows Thoth as the Ibis-headed scribe of the gods. (Ibises were considered sacred and were often mummified in Egyptian tradition.) Next to him is Am-mit, the eater of the dead. Am-mit is part crocodile, part lion and part hippopotamus. If the deceased does not pass the weighing of the soul, he/she is devoured by this monster. Thoth is shown recording the test results in his book. He also records all the deeds of a person throughout their life. He has been designated as a friend and guide of the deceased.

Illustration Eighteen: Thoth, Am-mit and Sesheta

Thoth is sometimes shown wearing a baboon's head, to symbolize the god of learning. (The Egyptians had a different concept of the baboon than the Western world.) But Thoth is most often depicted with the head of the Ibis, where his curved beak represents the crescent moon. He is identified by the Greeks as Hermes. Thoth was a judge in the quarrels between Horus and Set. It was believed that he was the son of Ra-Atum.

Thoth created writing in the form of hieroglyphics. Egyptian scribes used a form of pictorial writing along with 700 hieroglyphics. A shorthand version was used for writing documents. The finding of the Rosetta Stone in 1799 helped humanity to understand this important form of writing. The Rosetta Stone goes back to 195 B.C. The amazing thing about it was the inscriptions with a decree issued by Ptolemy V (205 to 180 B. C.). Furthermore, the decree was written in hieroglyphs in two languages: Greek and Demotic. Demotic, a simplified form of hieratic writing, was the popular language in Egypt in 195 B. C. Hieratic writing pertains to an abridged form of hieroglyphics, used by the priesthood in their records. This great discovery was a huge breakthrough in the deciphering of hieroglyphs, which, until this time, had all of the scholars puzzled.

As if to confirm the foregoing paragraph, an article written in Blavatsky's *The Theosophist*, Volume V, No. 1, dated October, 1883, entitled, "Was Writing Known Before Panini?" by "A Chela," provided a thought-provoking paragraph. It said that it could be proved that there existed two languages in every nation before the final division of languages. They were the popular language of the masses and the secret language of the initiates of the temple mysteries—the secret language being the universal language to which all could relate. It states that all great civilizations, such as the Egyptians, had its Demotic, as well as its Hieratic writing and language, resulting first in the pictorial writing of hieroglyphics, then later in a phonetic alphabet.

Thoth is the inventor of writing and lord of magic. He helped Isis restore and unify the scattered parts of Osiris with his magic. He is considered to be one of the oldest of the Egyptian gods. He is author of *The Book of the Dead*, god of Wisdom, Arbiter and Secretary to the gods as well as Codifier of Laws. My research finds that Thoth is often called the "Moon god," because he is known to guard the Moon and to measure time by the phases of the Moon. He also was the deputy of the Sun god, and was known as the messenger of the gods, just as Hermes and Mercury in Greek and Roman mythology, respectively. All in all, Thoth was a god of many talents.

Also shown with Thoth, in Illustration Eighteen, is his wife, Sesheta. She is goddess of mathematics, science and architecture. Her rule is over libraries and all literature. She has the honor of deciding the type of dwelling the soul deserves in the spiritual world. Sesheta is depicted with a panther skin dress, and a flower with seven petals that sit on top of her head. (Some sources consider the petals as seven stars.) On the roof of the Temple of Hathor at Dendera, the sign of Sagittarius is depicted wearing a crown.

What a comparison to the sign of Sagittarius! Sagittarians are often outspoken because of their accumulated knowledge, which gives them confidence. And they are very light-hearted in their sense of humor, although their blunt tongue can offend very sensitive types of people. Sagittarians are known for being great philosophers and teachers. In the ancient sacred teachings, the Sagittarian god-virtue is enthusiasm, represented by Zarathustra, who resided in the temple of Fire Beings, which was symbolically the sacred substance of the spirit nature of humanity. Zarathustras are beings who carried the spirit of fire to earth, and have authority over the fire element. They taught the religion of fire, which as been handed down through the ages in the East.

Medieval authorities held that Zarathustra was the son of Vesta, goddess of the galaxies, and the great salamander, Oromasis. For those who are wondering, "What is a salamander?" I refer you to Paracelsus, the Swiss-German doctor and alchemist, who taught that all of the four elements known as air, water, earth and fire, were two-fold in nature, and consisted of a vaporous, ghost-like substance. Therefore, fire is visible as well as invisible, with a spiritual flame penetrating through a physical flame. The invisible part of nature consists of elemental beings, divided into four categories: gnomes representing the earth, undines representing the water, sylphs representing the air, and salamanders representing fire. The Egyptians, as well as other ancient cultures, often mistook the salamanders for gods, because of the radiant splendor and power they emitted. The Greeks honored the fire spirits and kept incense burning on their altars perpetually. Ever since these ancient times, fires have burned on the altars in Persia in honor of Oromasis, Zarathustra's radiant father.

This is the period to pursue all types of knowledge, such as religion, esoteric studies, mythology, philosophy and psychology. Any spiritual studies can bring inspiration and awakenings now. The keywords for Sagittarius are stark honesty, idealism, and exploration. Jupiter is the ruler of this sign which stimulates expansion in higher learning, legal matters, publishing, intellectual matters, goals, future outlook and travel. Therefore, it is a good time to travel and expand your knowledge about other countries in order to understand your world better. The Sagittarius energy likes to grow in order to have more wisdom with which to philosophize and have debates with others. Do not forget to think before you speak. It follows that Sagittarius is straightforward and frank in pursuit of truth and justice. This is the time to seek inspiration for yourself and others. The charm of this sign is easy-going, optimistic and humorous with the big smile that wins many an admirer. This is the time to feel lucky and expansive, but be sure not to overrun the risks involved in betting, or any speculation. The enthusiasm of Sagittarius takes you to areas of adventure and a vision for the future.

CHAPTER FIFTEEN

CAPRICORN

"I am Hathor, lady of the sycamore."

The Egyptian month of Toobi covers the period of December 27 to January 25. This is the reign of the beautiful goddess, Hathor.

The glyph for Capricorn is symbolized by a stroke which introverts toward itself. This represents the self-scrutiny which Capricornians undergo as they express the path of the mind that seeks the infinite depths of the inner self.

Hathor was the Cow Goddess, most often portrayed with a crown of cow horns cupping the Sun. (SEE ILLUSTRATION NINETEEN.) She is the daughter of Re and Mut; her husband is Horus. Hathor had the high honor of being called the mother queen of all gods and goddesses.

Goddess of love, joy, music, dance, laughter and sensuality, Hathor was related to sex and fertility, and helped married women. At times she was depicted as a loving sacred cow, bringing nourishment and good news. From the Hathor sanctuary of Tuthmosis III, there is a sculpture of her grazing among the papyrus plants as a cow.

Illustration Nineteen: Hathor

Her temples were devoted to healing. However, at the time of the Egyptian New Year, the Dendera temple, the seat of worship of the goddess Hathor, became the scene of celebration and entertainment.

This description of Hathor does not sound like Capricorn at first. It sounds like Venus; in fact, the Greeks considered her as Aphrodite. So let us look at Venus in Capricorn. Venus in Capricorn is like reaching into the earth—at first, the soil is moist and cool—but at the center it is boiling fury and passion. The Capricorn goat is often conservative with material things, but pleasures are very important to him/her. That passion needs to be released. He/she also has the gift of perception, to bring the cherished goal into manifestation through inner powers that were developed after learning the lessons of life.

During this month, January 5th was observed as the day of Nilos. This was when the water of the Nile River was supposed to be at its purest point. Ephiphanius wrote that this was the time when water was withdrawn from the river and stored in Egypt and the surrounding countries. According to myth, some springs and rivers turned into wine on January 6th. In Catholic communities, priests still bestow blessings on rivers and other bodies of water at this season of the year, a practice that is derived from this ancient Egyptian custom.

From the research that is available on Hathor, I see her as one of the most influential of the pantheon of gods. From the book, *The Hathor Material*, by Tom Kenyon and Virginia Essene, the name Hathor has even greater meaning. According to the authors, the Hathors are the name for an ascended intergalactic civilization that assisted ancient civilizations such as Egypt and Tibet. The Hathors are masters of love, sound and joy, who have chosen Virginia Essene as a channel to relay their messages to humanity in this current evolution. Many tombs of the pharaohs include the description of "seven Hathors," who predict the fate of a child at birth. Could the Hathors be the figures depicted on the Temple of Isis on the Island of Philae, and at the Temple of Hathor in Dendera?

I would dare to speculate that they could be. To some readers, this may seem "way out." However, when you study the faces of the beings on the columns at Dendera and the Temple of Isis on Philae Island, you get the feeling that this truly has the ring of another dimension. How many people on the planet earth have pointed ears? These statues were created long before Star Trek and Mister Spock. (See Illustration Six again.)

From what I understand of *The Hathor Material,* artisians, of the early times before the pharaohs, sculpted representations of the Hathors on temple walls and at the tops of columns.

While some sources consider Sekhmet and Bastet to be a facet of Hathor, I disagree with these sources. The confusion seems to lie with an association of Hathor with lions, like the mother goddess of the Sumerian pantheon, Ninhursaga, who was also a healer. Sekhmet was married to Ptah, and Hathor was married to Horus. I believe that Hathor is the celestial representation, and that Sekhmet and Bastet were a physical representation of the more human, animal qualities. Hathor has a divine connection as the daughter of Rah.

This period of the calendar is beneficial for concentrating on new business tactics, career undertakings, improving your image, profession, and the all-important task of making your mark in the world. The keywords of Capricorn are diligence, ambition and conscience. This is a great time for laying foundations for the future by setting goals and ideals to follow through in a methodical fashion, in order to turn your dreams into reality. This is a time of achievement and recognition, meeting influential people and learning how to delegate certain duties and responsibilities. The Capricorn energy is disciplined, practical and stable in order to create security for the future. Determined and hardworking, Capricorns need to establish a goal, without which they are lost. They need order to feel complete, while they travel down their daily to-do list. There is respect for authority, and Capricorns admire the wisdom of age and experience in others. Beneath the reserved exterior is a unique sense of humor, plus an inner strength that comes from experience and discipline.

CHAPTER SIXTEEN

AQUARIUS

"I am Amun-Rah, King of the gods."

This is the period from January 26 to February 24, and the month is called Mechir.

The glyph for Aquarius is two wavy lines which symbolize the flow of knowledge and energy. This is often compared to electrical currents, because the perceptions of the the Aquarian are as rapid as lightening.

This is the reign of Amun-Rah, Lord of the heavens, King of the gods and Light of the world. From the time of the Middle Kingdom, Amun (the hidden one) was honored and merged with Rah (the approachable one). In ILLUSTRATION TWENTY, he is seen with a crown that is representative of Upper Egypt. He is carrying a scepter and an ankh, which all primary gods and goddesses carry.

The myth says that Amun-Rah was self-created, rising out of the primal waters as a child on a lotus. Originally, Rah was the solar god, god of all gods. Then the Egyptians combined him with Amun, making him Amun-Rah. When he became linked with Rah, the ancient sun god, he then rose to chief deity of the Middle and New Kingdom. They built his temple at Karnak. More than 2,000 years in the making, containing 130 pillars, encompassing 247 acres, Karnak is considered the largest religious site on the planet. It is located in Luxor, which was called Thebes in olden times. Amun is the invisible creative power of all life, and is represented as a beetle, a man, a falcon and the Sun. Sometimes he is shown with the Sun disk upon a human form. His god-virtues to help the earth during the month of Mechir are leadership, confidence, discretion and creativity.

Illustration Twenty: Amun-Rah

A statue of Amun-Rah shows him with an erect phallus and one arm raised up, as the symbol of the god of fertility. In the Pharaonic Divinity myth, it says that when Amun-Rah saw the beautiful queen of Egypt, he took on the appearance of her husband to seduce her. The queen conceived a child who was destined to become the next king of Egypt. The child and its soul were formed on the potter's wheel of Khnum. Then Amun-Rah accepted the child as his own. The purpose of this myth was to legitimize the rise of Queen Hatshepsut to the throne as pharaoh, instead of her nephew, Thutmosis, III. This is depicted in the temple at Luxor in the birthing house, which is a part of most major Egyptian temples.

The goddess Mut is the wife of Amun, and is known as the Mother of the world, and Queen of all goddesses. Sometimes Mut is depicted with a double crown on her head, sometimes as a vulture, or sometimes as a lioness-headed goddess. She is the ruler of Karnak and the third member of the Divine Triad. (The Divine Trio of Thebes consisted of Amun-Rah, Mut and their son, Khonsu, called "the Traverser," since his name means "wanderer." The number three was significant to the Egyptians. Their daughters were Hathor and Maat.)

During the Egyptian Opet Festival, Amun-Rah with his wife, Mut, and son, Khonsu, were carried by a procession from the Karnak temple to the Luxor temple, considered to be approximately one mile along the designated road between the two temples. At one time, this was a long avenue of stone ram-headed sphinxes, which lined each side of the road from Karnak to Luxor. Some of these sphinxes still remain at the entrance of the Karnak Temple.

The sphinx-lined avenue was designed so that on the twenty-first of June, when the sun reached its farthest point northward, its rays spread down the long avenue. These rays passed through the temple entrance, and, for a brief moment, illuminated the sacred image in the Holy of Holies area at Karnak. This was a symbolic impregnation of fertile seed in the womb of Mother Earth by the Sun. Every temple in Egypt has a sacred Holy of Holies chamber.

Amun-Rah, Mut and Khonsu were carried in processional barques towed by priests. Upon reaching Luxor, a symbolized marriage was performed between Amun-Rah and Mut, which led to her conceiving Anero, the reigning king. This confirmed his right to rule, and represented the myth of the divine king. This festival survives to the present day through the procession of the Muslim saint, Abu el-Haggag.

This is the time of the year to make changes in order to be open to new opportunities, new experiences and new friendships. The keywords for Aquarius are humanitarianism, independence, and detachment. Group activities, intellectual pursuits, and not being afraid to take risks are indicated now. It's a good time to investigate ancient teachings, astrology, and esoteric knowledge, anything that is unique, unconventional and stimulating. Let the world know that you have unusual talents to share. Allow yourself to be spontaneous, so that you can get out of the rut of old routines. You can increase your income during this period by letting those in power know of your special aims. Choose friends who can help you boost humanitarian projects. The Aquarian energy is good for developing social contacts, profiting from business and concentrating on your hopes and wishes. Uranus, the ruling planet, bestows the gifts of perception of future societal trends, and the need for freedom. Humanitarian awareness enables you to work for universal goals in the big picture of life, as well as being friendly and helpful to individual strangers. The electric quality of Aquarius can manifest as intuition and a genius that can be unpredictable, while at the same time inventive.

CHAPTER SEVENTEEN

PISCES

"I am Osiris, Lord of Amentel (the underworld)."

The month Phamenoth runs from February 25 to March 26.

The glyph for Pisces is symbolized by two fish that are joined by a cord, even though they are facing opposite directions. It represents a combination of two modes of life, or alternating motion from above to below and vice-versa. This gives Pisces a wide range of motion, as the personality learns to evolve and grow and find a resolution to the duality of the world and to link the earth with the heavens. And when this happens, Pisces comes into discovering completeness with Universal Spirit.

This is the reign of Osiris, god of the spirit world. He is the most renowned of all Egyptian gods because of his unique status, and his generous, kind, peaceful manner. He was the sun of Geb (earth) and Nut (sky). Osiris and Isis ruled as king and queen of Egypt, teaching many arts and crafts to the people, such as agriculture, weaving, cooking, writing and reading. Then Osiris decided to bring the culture of Egypt to other parts of the world.

SPECIAL NOTE: I want to insert here some interesting information from the book, *Life and Teachings of the Masters of the Far East* by Baird T. Spalding who traveled to the Himalayas, the

Gobi Desert, and various places in the Far East. The purpose is to follow through with the thought that some of the gods of Egypt were once real people. Spalding wrote about a priest, a follower of Thoth, who taught the Egyptians about the pure, spiritual teachings of Osiris. However, the dynasties following the time of Thoth proceeded to follow the teachings of the Black Magicians of Egypt instead. Their kingdom fell as they abandoned the higher teachings. The actual Osiris was born in Atlantis over thirty-five thousand years ago. He was a descendent of the illumined elders of higher thought. Many years after Osiris died, he was called a god because of his teachings and magical works. The chronologists began making images of Osiris as a god, and they promoted him to a King. The Osiris teachings came from his forefathers in the land of Lemuria. Osiris was sent to Lemuria to study in his younger years. Then he returned to his homeland to become the leader of the Atlanteans. While he was in Lemuria, the people had fallen back to following the dark forces. But upon his return he brought his people back to the worship of God within, the I AM Presence of God, through meditation techniques.

Now back to the legend.

While Osiris traveled to Asia, Isis was assigned to rule in his place. Upon his return, the evil brother, Set, invited him to a feast. Now we have the test I outlined in a previous chapter. Set displayed a chest, and said he would offer it to anyone who could fit inside. After everyone at the feast tried the chest, Osiris went inside and fit perfectly, of course, because it had been built for him by Set. As soon as Osiris was inside, the lid was slabbed down, nailed tight, and thrown into the Nile, thereby drowning Osiris.

The chest carrying Osiris floated into the Mediterranean Sea. Upon landing in Byblos, Lebanon, it became lodged in a tree. The grief of Isis was so great that her tears flooded the Nile. She wandered everywhere in search of Osiris, and she was assisted by Anubis, who could track down anything. After they arrived in Byblos, Isis noticed a strange column cut from a tree. She perceived by the scent that this held the body of Osiris. Isis eventually got the king to give her the column, which contained the chest holding Osiris. She brought it back to Egypt, and with the assistance of her sister, Nephthys, Isis was magically turned into a swallow. The bird flapped its wings and stirred the air to bring breath into the lungs of Osiris. When he was revived, she used this opportunity to conceive her son, Horus. (This was considered an Immaculate Conception.) Then she protected Horus by hiding him in a thicket of papyrus, and guarded the tomb of Osiris.

One evening, Isis went to check on Horus, thereby leaving the tomb unguarded. Set had been waiting for this chance. He opened the coffin of Osiris and hacked it into fourteen pieces, scattering the pieces all over Egypt. Isis was able to retrieve all parts of Osiris except the penis, which had been swallowed by a fish. She brought all pieces together to the island of Philae. With the special help of Anubis, Osiris became the first mummy. Therefore, Osiris became king of the underworld, or heaven. Of all Egyptians, no god has had such a wide influence as Osiris, the resurrection god. And Isis, the one who revives, became the savior of her husband.

In ILLUSTRATION TWENTY-ONE, Osiris is shown with his wife, Isis, and her sister, Nephthys. Osiris has the flail and the crook in his hands, which are symbols of guidance and discipline. Osiris achieved the position of god of the underworld (heaven) after he was killed by his brother, Set.

As god of the underworld, the celestial counterpart of Osiris became Orion, a constellation that the ancient Egyptians knew as *Sah*, and depicted as the three belt stars. Thus, the constellation of Orion was Osiris's connection to the stars—his soul connection. The Egyptians considered Orion as the soul of Osiris. Orion is the Shepherd of Heaven and the Great Initiator.

The Alpha star of Orion, situated on its right shoulder, is the fixed star, Betelgeuse, meaning "the Announcer" in Arabic. Fixed stars have a divine purpose in bringing out the karmic patterns of individuals, since their magnetic energies interchange with the inhabitants of earth. The ancients knew that higher truths were encoded in star patterns. For example, "As above, so below" is often quoted from Hermes. Buildings of the ancients encoded star patterns and significant astronomical cycles within the physical layout of a building. *The Orion Mystery* co-authored by

Robert Bauval and Adrian Gilbert, presents research saying that the pyramids of Giza were built to correspond to the constellation Orion. Orion was a part of the initiations held in the Great Pyramid. (This makes sense to me from the standpoint that initiations were held in the Great Pyramid, as recorded in ancient teachings such as the Rosicrucians.) This will be explained more on the information below about the Hermetic texts and the Duat.

Illustration Twenty-one: Osiris, Isis and Nephthys

This research coincides with what Edgar Cayce said in his readings, that the position of Orion in 10,500 B.C. was stellar to an important pattern between the Great Pyramid and Orion, and that this was the time when the Atlanteans came to Egypt to preserve their records. Cayce said that, prior to 10,000 B.C., ten Atlanteans were led by Iltar to the Yucatan area of Mexico, where they built a temple, similar to the one in Giza, to house Atlantean records.

Osiris is compared to the sign of Pisces. His message is that rebirth follows death. He guides humanity through the different phases of life. He can also help a soul enter the underworld, like a guiding savior.

This is the time period to program yourself for meditation and dream analysis, to help you get in touch with your intuitive level of understanding. The keywords for Pisces are receptivity, imagination and compassion. The Piscean energy is a very mystical, highly developed sensitive nature. Pisceans are always receiving impressions from the outer environment, and may not be completely aware of the important impressions until they learn to work with dreams and meditation. Just before bedtime, tell yourself before you prepare for sleep, that you will remember your dreams. Then write down any recall of those dreams upon awakening, for special insight and guidance. Take time to listen to inspiring music, such as classical music. You may feel like drawing, painting or writing. Just set your imagination free, and see what develops. Learn to enjoy the creative process, and surprise yourself. Your connection to the spiritual realms and your angelic guides is often strengthened during this time. Psychic abilities and healing powers may be heightened during this period. The Pisces energy is spent helping others most of the time throughout the year. But this is the time to go within and discover your own treasures so that you can replenish and go back to serving again with more strength and that Pisces patience when duty calls.

Ancient civilizations viewed Noah and the Great Flood as a myth to signify salvation for the earth so that it could begin a new era. It was suggested that the sign of Pisces reflected the symbolism of Noah, which represented the transition between two ages, namely, Pisces and

Aquarius, and saving what was necessary to bring it into the new age of Aquarius with hope for peace and a better world.

This concludes the zodiac of the most important gods. These super beings possessed many talents and sometimes conflicting roles. However, they all represented a central theme to all Egyptians. They sustained a belief in God and the people that "You will not disappear." Egyptians believed that the preservation of a name insured the preservation of the being. It was their conviction that to speak of the dead was to make them live again. In Egypt, it is common to find fathers, mothers and children picnicking on Fridays, or some special holiday, among the graves of their ancestors.

CHAPTER EIGHTEEN

REVELATIONS THROUGH THE HERMETIC TEXTS AND THE MYSTERIOUS CHAMBERS ABOVE THE KING'S CHAMBER

<u>The Hermetic Texts</u>

In the Egyptian city of Alexandria, an enormous amount of effort has gone into the reconstruction of the Library of Alexandria, which opened in October, 2002. (We lost at least 532,000 documents containing ancient spiritual traditions when the original library at Alexandria was burned.) The reconstruction has produced a storehouse of exquisite treasures of knowledge. I *w*as in complete awe when I entered this library. One of the most famous components of the library is entitled, "Ancient History." An ancient body of writings in Greek, the predominant influence in the Ptolemic era, gives sky-to-ground connections which are linked to resurrection and immortality, an important subject to both Greeks and Egyptians. The ancient writings were called "Hermetic Texts," which were the work of the god known as Thoth (Hermes per the Greek version), who was probably a real person, as well as Osiris, also noted to be an actual person. In my book, *Mystical Secrets of the Stars,* I explained how the myths of the gods had their basis in real-life people and situations.

In one passage of the "Hermetic Texts," Thoth tells Asclepius (who later became the Greek god of healing): "Do you not know, Asclepius, that Egypt is an image of heaven? Or, so to speak more exactly, in Egypt all the operations of the powers which rule and work in heaven have been transferred down to earth below?" These powers were given to help the initiate achieve immortality.

According to the teachings of the Rosicrucians, the Great Pyramid played a great part in this initiation held in the King's Chamber. Citing *The Book of the Dead,* it was necessary for the initiate to verify his integrity and courage *before* being admitted into the Grand Gallery in the Great Pyramid. The Grand "Galleria" is called the Hall of Truth in Light and the Crossing of the Waters of Life. This must be the reason why travelers to the Great Pyramid often face challenges, as if to prove worthy of entering this mind-boggling site. (Personally, I missed the flight where I was to join the tour group I was traveling with. Besides some physical problem, I continued on, in spite of the drawbacks, and was able to join the group the next day.) Others have had challenges from hospital stays to leg injuries, and the list goes on. Events will happen to test a person's commitment before entering the Holy of Holies, be it the Great Pyramid, Saqquara, Dendera, or any temple in Egypt, where there could be an initiation for the traveler who has a spiritual leaning in their heart.)

After reaching the top of the ascending passage in the Grand Gallery, the initiate reaches a stone cube called the Great Step. Then there is the Ante Chamber, which leads to the King's Chamber. The Ante Chamber is referred to as the Room of the Veils. This is a very low passage, which requires the initiate to duck or crawl through the area. It represents a space to receive an understanding of the mysteries of life which were not entirely clear to the initiate beforehand, and the veils are lifted. The initiate then proceeds to the King's Chamber, where he prepares to go before the Great Judge. This is represented in the Tarot cards as the Hierophant.

It has been said that our journey on the Earth plane is to learn to master the principles found in the Tarot cards. In my book, *Mystical Secrets of the Stars,* I give the Major Arcana cards that correspond to each Zodiac sign. Here is a quote from my book:

"The Tarot's original Major Arcana of twenty-two cards were large tapestries in a secret passage between the Sphinx and the Great Pyramid of Egypt. The initiates walked through the passageway to receive inspiration from the symbols and the pictures.

"The Tarot card form was created after the decimation of the libraries of Alexandria, Egypt. Because of this great loss, certain members of the Brotherhood of Light moved to Fez, Morocco and designed the Tarot deck to preserve some of the mysterious teachings previously housed in the Alexandrian libraries. Down through time, the deck has undergone changes and was made available to the public."

The Major Arcana Card Number Five is the Hierophant. In Hermetic initiations, it represents the neophyte on the spiritual path who has been brought before Osiris to receive his blessing. While in the King's Chamber, the neophyte can hear the chants of the ancient Egyptian Temple choir. (Each one of us on our Egyptian tour took our turn to lie down in the sarcophagus in the King's Chamber. While here, many of us heard chanting very similar to the Gregorian chant.)

During the time in the sarcophagus, the initiate perceives that he is experiencing an integration of the male and female aspects within, a balancing of the yin/yang, where there is no longer duality. The Hierophant card has two figures that appear before the Hierophant for his blessing which leads to the union of the body with the spirit in universal consciousness. Plato and Jesus have been purported to experience this mystical event in the Great Pyramid.

The King's Chamber is the highest chamber in the Great Pyramid. It represents the conquering of death by life, and victory over ignorance. It was called the Room of the Mystery of the Open Tomb and Room of Judgment and the Purification of Nations. The initiate appeared before the Great Judge in a spiritual sense. The red granite sarcophagus played an important role. It is in the King's Chamber without a lid. This is where the inductee went through the initiation of raising the body through a kundalini technique.

Iamblichus, an initiate of the Brotherhood of Light in the 4th Century, wrote a document, "An Egyptian Initiation." This document depicts the trials the initiate must successfully pass in order to be equipped to qualify for initiations into the Mysteries of Egypt. The neophyte was taken to an underground hall between the Sphinx and the Great Pyramid, where he had to memorize twenty-two tapestries hanging on the wall. These represented the twenty-two pictures of the Major Arcana of the Tarot. The initiate had to understand the symbolism of these pictorial tapestries, as well as certain astrological symbols in order to pass the initiations which opened the door to the great mysteries of life and resurrection. (See the Appendix of astrological symbols at the end of this book.)

The Mysterious Hidden Chambers

Although the King's Chamber is the highest functional chamber in the Great Pyramid, there are hidden chambers above it which have long been considered a mystery.

These five hidden chambers are horizontal chambers with low ceilings, situated on top of each other, directly above the King's Chamber. However, Egyptologists have questioned for years why these chambers are located here with no known function. This has been one of the most contested aspects of the construction of the Great Pyramid.

There is speculation that they were constructed to relieve the tons of pressure upon the King's Chamber. These so-called "relieving chambers" were not designed with an entrance to go inside. Derek Hitchins, a British systems engineer, in 2015 wrote that the reason for these chambers is difficult to explain because their layers of granite bear down on the walls of the King's Chamber underneath them. Since their structure places a large load on the walls, this could not have a relieving function.

In 1765 a traveler, only known as "Davidson," found a small, rough passage to the lowest chamber. But he found no markings on the walls of the chamber to give any hint of its purpose. Then in 1837 Howard Vyse and J.S. Perring forged a tunnel into the upper chambers where they found red hieroglyphs on the walls. The hieroglyphs were within an oval cartouche. A cartouche is an oval tablet with scroll work on it. This is often found on ancient monuments with scrollwork expressing royal names. The cartouches contained two names, "Khufu" and "Khnum-Khuf."

Khufu was a king of the Fourth Dynasty, and scholars say that Khnum-Khuf signifies a god. Egyptologists say that Khufu and Khnum-Khuf are two different names for the same god. Khufu's name existed on many monuments as a sacred sign of protection. It was standard practice for kings to bear the names of the gods they portrayed. The words, "Khnumu-Khufui" means "the god Khnum protects me." I venture to say that there is a special purpose for the representation of Khnum in the Great Pyramid.

Let us remember that Khnum was the lord of creation. He was depicted with a "was" in his left hand and an ankh in his right hand. The ankh represents everlasting life. It is feasible that he was a part of the initiation of ascension which took place in the Great Pyramid. He was invoked to protect the initiates as they went through the ritual and to ease them into everlasting life. And Osiris was invoked to lead them into the doorway to higher dimensions.

As we ponder whether or not the relieving chambers had something to do with initiations, let us consider what John Davis wrote in his book, *Be the Light of the World*. John Davis is the Director of the Coptic Fellowship International, a philosophy based upon the Egyptian Mystery Schools. He is the successor of the Egyptian Master Hamid Bey, who founded the Coptic Fellowship of America. In his book, Mr. Davis specifies the Great Pyramid as the place of the ritual of the ascension of a Master's soul from the physical body into a body of light. Seven High Priests/Masters conducted the ritual. The body was placed in the sarcophagus in the King's Chamber. The ascension ritual lasted three days and three nights. One of the seven Masters, the Golden Master, entered a special chamber above the King's Chamber, as a part of this secret ritual. Archeologists have never been able to determine which chamber this could be.

The Sacred Duat

In ancient funerary texts which even pre-date the "Hermetic Texts," we learn of "Shat Ent Am Duat," which means "The Book of What is in the Duat," where the initiate is instructed to build an exact replica on the ground corresponding to the sky called, "the hidden circle of the

Duat." The Duat is a star within a circle. And the text basically says that whoever can make an exact copy of this star shall be a spirit equipped in both heaven and earth. The Duat sky region was predominated by Orion and Leo, apparently imaged on the ground at Giza in the southern shaft of the King's Chamber in the Great Pyramid. The corridors and chambers of the pyramid systems are akin to the vignettes of the Eighteenth Dynasty tomb walls representing regions of the Duat. The mysterious reference to the "Kingdom of Sokar in the Fifth Dimension of the Duat" left me aghast, as it told that this was the way into the holy country where travelers enter the hidden place of the sacred Duat. Upon further research, I found that Sokar was considered an aspect of Horus, the son of the god of life everlasting who makes the way for humanity, much like Jesus, the Son of God. In addition, Horus was considered the second aspect of the Trinity, like Jesus.

This hidden holy place of the Duat sky area in Parts III and IV of the Hermetic texts was clearly described as the constellation of Orion and Leo and the star Sirius. It also describes the time when the gods came to earth to establish their kingdom in Egypt. These gods were Thoth, Hathor, Osiris, Isis and Horus. Let us remember that Osiris was the king who was killed and given rebirth in order to have everlasting life as the Lord of the Duat. The Duat, the star within a circle, represented the King being guided to the celestial dwelling place of Orion. The Duat also means a dual pattern showing that earth connects to heaven. The Duat is the doorway to the Fifth and higher dimensions. On the Summer Solstice, as the sun appeared on the horizon, the constellation of Orion and the star Sirius became enwrapped by the Duat. As the glow of dawn increased, the stars seemed to be swallowed up. The ancients saw this as a symbol of purification and the ascension to a higher dimension.

> "There is a path by which God may be reached if one's heart is ready to tread it. The path of initiation leads to union with God."
>
> --Ascended Master Serapis Bey

CHAPTER NINETEEN

> "The excellence of the soul is understanding; for the man who understands is conscious, devoted, and already god-like."
>
> --Thoth-Hermes Trismegistus

THOTH-HERMES TRISMEGISTUS—EMBODIMENT OF THE UNIVERSAL MIND

So much has been mentioned thus far on Thoth/Hermes, but we have only just begun to even tap the voluminous meaning and influence of this extraordinary being. Hermes was called "The Three Times Greatest" because he was revered as the greatest of all philosophers, the greatest of all priests, and the greatest of all kings.

Some of the knowledge that the great Hermes released to humanity included medicine, chemistry, alchemy, astrology, law, art, music, philosophy, geography, mathematics, anatomy, and the art of communication. He was considered the master of all arts and sciences.

Iamblichus claimed that Hermes wrote twenty thousand books which seems like a monumental task for even a master soul like Hermes, who was identified with the early sages and prophets. Moreover, Hermes is known as the author of books from the Historic Period when books were written only on papyrus.

The ancient alchemists called their chemical writings, "hermetic" which contained astrological symbols, for example, Venus, or Mercury. The phrase, "Hermetically Sealed" refers to the closing of a glass container by fusion.

Paracelsus often referred to hermetic medicines and the Freemasonry of the Middle Ages as heavily involved in hermetic terminology.

The artist J. A. Knapp painted an intriguing rendering of Hermes standing on the back of Typhon, the dragon of perversion. In this painting, Hermes represents Universal Wisdom as he overcomes the horrific Typhon. To the initiates of Egyptian Mysteries, Typhon was the devourer of souls. He represented the lowest of earth entities that swallowed the imperfect individual who had to return from the spiritual plane to the physical plane again because of accumulated negative karma. To be released from the cycle of rebirth and the swallowing of Typhon, one had to learn how to defeat the enemy.

Knapp's rendering of Hermes is a most fascinating depiction of him holding the caduceus, the ancient winged rod with two serpents entwined (often seen as the medical symbol) in his left hand. Then on his right hand stands the immortal Emerald Tablet that is recorded in Mayan and Rosicrucian teachings, as a significant philosophical stone. Even more interesting, Hermes wears the symbolic Masonic apron which appears in the temples of Egypt, such as Saqquara. On the edge of the apron are two small circles, representing Hermes. Around the right side of the head of Hermes, a circle is drawn, containing the ibis, a sacred bird to the Egyptians, and often associated with the Egyptian medical arts. It was common for Egyptian priests to wear masks of the ibis head to represent Hermes and/or Thoth throughout initiation ceremonies.

In this Knapp painting, we also can see another circle that depicts a dog on the lower left side of Hermes, because of the devotion and intelligence associated with the qualities of Hermes and man's best friend. The Uraeus, the serpent symbol, depicts the regeneration of the lower power of the dragon that lies beneath the foot of Hermes. The Uraeus is seen on the forehead of Hermes, as it is seen on the forehead of the Pharaoh who has undergone the required initiation to raise the kundalini energy. An interesting white band with the figure of a scarab lies over the heart of Hermes, signifying the presence of the spiritual light within his soul. The tail of the terrible Typhon has three arrows which typify the three destructive unfoldments of universal energy; namely, physical, mental, and moral perversion. This entire work of art speaks about the mastery of life that can be achieved by the transmutation of the physical body, the illumination of the mental body, and the regeneration of the emotional body.

CHAPTER TWENTY

THE MYSTERIOUS TEMPLE AT DENDERA, EGYPT

The famous Zodiac of Dendera, one of the oldest known of all zodiacs, was originally believed to pre-date the Christian Era by 5,000 years or more, and has long been a source of mystery. After a carbon-14 analysis, the original viewpoint was highly considered. However, there has been a wide debate as to the correct historical data. It has been often believed that the zodiac itself began in Egypt. In fact, it was the Egyptians who created a zodiac with each of the twelve signs divided into three ten-degree units called decanates, each governed by a different planet.

The unusual circular zodiac at Dendera was discovered in more modern times during Napoleon's campaign. When Napoleon arrived at Dendera, it was filled with sand, more than halfway up to the temple ceilings. In 1798, Napoleon brought a team of 165 scientists to record drawings of the Sphinx and the Great Pyramid. Because of this, it was said that modern Egyptology was founded by Napoleon in 1798 A. D.

After Napoleon's campaign, many Egyptian artifacts disappeared, ending up in European institutions. Moreover, the sites where unique Egyptian objects had been originally, were left with only copies. The French had something to do with the removal of the original Zodiac of Dendera. This famous astrological relief was taken by the French in 1820 from the roof chapel ceiling at Dendera and moved to the Louvre in Paris. The zodiac existing now at the roof chapel in Dendera is a blackened plaster cast of the original, and it is the only circular zodiac in Egypt.

The ancient village of Dendera is sixty miles south of Abydos and thirty miles north of Luxor. This quaint little place is on the west bank of the Nile River, opposite Qena. It stands on the site of ancient Tentyra, formerly the capital of the sixth province of Upper Egypt.

Similar to many temples in Egypt, Dendera was built upon previously existing temples. In one of its underground crypts an inscription states that the temple had been built according to a specific plan written in ancient script upon a scroll from the time of the "Companions of Horus." I found this particularly intriguing, because this confirmed other sources that said that there was a time when the "Companions of Horus" ruled Egypt, in the prehistoric era, as recorded on fragmentary Egyptian chronological tables. This means the "Companions of Horus" would have been in a time prior to Dynastic Egypt. (SEE ILLUSTRATION TWENTY-TWO.)

Illustration Twenty-two: Companions of Horus

This would also give credence to the Cosmic Beings of Hathor, who once were an influence in prehistoric Egypt, and could be the beings portrayed on the columns at Dendera and on the Island of Philae. Artifacts from the Old Kingdom (2575 B. C. to 2175 B. C.) have been found at Dendera. In addition, evidence from a reused block of an artifact from the Middle Kingdom (from 1975 B. C. to 1640 B. C.) depicts Pharaoh Amenemhet I. It serves as a water spout, with an inscription calling attention to an earlier time in history. There is no doubt that these images were derived from the most ancient tradition, making the Dendera Zodiac the most fascinating of Egyptian temples from the venerable past.

Now, to make this even more amazing, Fred Gettings, in *The Arkana Dictionary of Astrology* cites research suggesting that the Temple of Hathor at Dendera, with its unusual round constellation map, was based on prototypes from 2900 B.C., showing that this astrological expression had been preserved in the Ancient Egyptian Mysteries. The Dendera images and symbols are undoubtedly derived from a most ancient tradition which, in effect, makes the Dendera Zodiac one of the most attention-getting astrological survivals from the past.

The Dendera temple dedicated to Hathor was originally erected by Khufu, the pharaoh of the Fourth Dynasty (2590 to 2568 B. C.) It was replaced by Pepi I of the Sixth Dynasty (2327 to 2278 B. C.), followed by Amenemhet I of the Twelfth Dynasty (1991 to 1962 B. C.) and finally by Thutmose III of the Eighteenth Dynasty (1490 to 1436 B. C.).

The way the *present* temple exists was initially built in the first century B. C. under the rule of the last Ptolemies. Then it was finished under Augustus (30 B. C. to 14 A. D.). The cost of such temples was extravagant in those times, and it took years to complete them.

Dendera was the main temple of the goddess Hathor. The name of Hathor means "House of Horus" and we know that Hathor was the wife (consort) of the god Horus of Edfu. Every year there was an enormous festival where worshippers traveled between the Temple of Edfu and the Temple of Dendera in honor of these two deities. At one point in history, Horus and his wife,

Hathor, led a procession between the two temples and underwent initiations of strict fasting and other abstentions before the glorious feast of joyful celebration and the drinking of wine.

A Miraculous Healing Center

At one point in time, Dendera was a healing center, much like a modern hospital, where people journeyed to take part in therapies, and some miraculous cures were reportedly performed for pilgrims there. It became well-known as a place where magical therapies were conducted. It was also a place to come for negativities to be removed.

Sacred Teachings were Encoded

As events drew near for Egyptian customs to give way to Ptolemaic times, the guardians of traditional wisdom knew that their ancient system was winding down. In order to preserve the Egyptian sacred writings from desecration or destruction, they proceeded to enshrine certain texts on the walls of the newly designed temples. Thus, they were available to be seen by the public, but at the same time encoded so that only the astute scholars would know of its true meaning.

The encoding of hieroglyphs became a problem when the Ptolemies devised a complex system of symbols unknown by previous Old and Middle Kingdom scholars. Therefore, the former secret texts were understandable to only specially trained priests and scribes. However, because of the enshrined texts on the wall of the temples, serious Egyptian scholars were able to translate Egyptian myths, rites and ceremonies that may have otherwise been lost. Intensive work by Egyptological specialists is still being done to transcribe such texts.

A Walk through the Temple

The front entrance of the Temple of Dendera is unlike any other Egyptian temple, not pyramid shaped nor a pylon-marked gateway. A few stray dogs wander around, while some vendors display some shawls or shirts, with their children offering little paper fans, or wheat fans to bring good luck.

The visitor approaches a long walkway through an enclosure where a statue of the god Bes awaits off to the left of the entrance. Although Bes is not a member of the Pantheon of gods, he is the god of childbirth and patron of music and laughter. He is seen as a dwarf with a beard, long hair and a tail. (SEE ILLUSTRATION TWENTY-THREE.)

Ugly gods had the purpose of frightening away evil spirits. The ugly dwarf, Bes, in conjunction with the goddess Tauret, helped mothers giving birth. Bes was popular with married couples, who often displayed his statue in their homes because of the good fortune he was supposed to bring to families. The ghastly appearance of Tauret also had the effect of chasing evil spirits away. Because of this, pregnant women wore the charm of Tauret around their necks to insure safety for themselves and their unborn child.

The long walkway leads through the courtyard to six columns that outline the front of the temple with heads of the goddess Hathor to greet the visitor. (Refer back to Illustration Six.)

Illustration Twenty-three: Bes

The most interesting part of this temple is its ceilings. Like most of the Egyptian temples along the Nile, the ceilings are decorated with astronomical and astrological symbols, as well as the gods and goddesses connected to this vast array. For example, the third aisle inward through the entrance of Dendera, gives a lovely representation on the ceiling of the Sky Goddess Nut, elongating her body over the twelve signs of the zodiac, as well other constellations.

A doorway to the Temple of Dendera leads into a six-columned Hypostyle Hall, with sanctuaries on the right and on the left (hypostyle means having many columns to support the roof). The uppermost parts of the columns have sculptured heads of Hathor surrounded with vegetable foliage. This artwork of the harvest vegetables is typical of Ptolemaic art, making this temple different from temples of earlier origin.

The columns are set upon granite drums, possibly because granite is a fire symbol to Egyptians, and the granite drums could symbolize the fiery nature of the goddess Hathor. To the left of the Hypostyle entrance, the king consecrates the temple to the lovely Hathor. This Hypostyle Hall was called the Hall of Appearances, because during the processionals, the statue of Hathor was carried from the subterranean crypts, making her appear here. Aisle Seven of this hall has a laboratory that concocted recipes for perfumes and oils used in the temple ceremonies. Essentials oils were highly developed and used for medicinal and pleasurable purposes by the Egyptians; however, much of this craft was lost through the ages. The passageway from Aisle 11 led to the sacred well, always a component of the major temples to furnish the purified water for ceremonies by the priests, the king and, often, his queen.

The next entrance is into the Hall of Offerings. This is where the Egyptians celebrated the taming of the lioness, and the priest offered a song to Horus and Hathor. From the Hall of Offerings, the Hall of Ennead is reached. On the festival days, it was here that the pantheon of gods who were related to Hathor came to join in the celebration.

The Hall of Offerings leads into the Sanctuary, which is the "Holy of Holies." The inscriptions refer to this part of the temple as the Hidden Chamber. Here was kept the images of Hathor. Only the king and his priest were allowed into this chamber, once a year on the birthday of Hathor, which was the New Year in July. The performance of specific rites of this festival is inscribed on the walls. It describes the time of Horus and Hathor when they entered this sanctuary alone and fasted for so many hours.

The Sanctuary is encircled with a number of dark chapels leading off its central location. This has been referred to as the Mysterious Corridor, which contains pictorial reliefs devoted to Isis, Sokar, Harsomtus (Ihy), son of Horus and Hathor. The gods of Lower Egypt are also represented, along with the sacred sistrum of Hathor.

As I mentioned previously, Sokar was the hawk-god, who was identified, in some cases, with Horus. Sokar made silver bowls for the deceased to bathe their feet. He mixed herbs and spices to make ointments for funerary rites. Sokar was also identified with Ptah because he was a craftsman. Sokar is often depicted traveling in his boat as Lord of the Mysterious Region.

One chapel, Aisle 25, was the container for the "menat," Hathor's special necklace that could balance any power or opposing force. This necklace, combined with the sistrum, played an important role in the understanding of the vibrations of music, and how it related to cosmic harmony.

A Healing Takes Place

In back of the Holy of Holies and the Mysterious Corridor is a very interesting feature of underground crypts. A few of these crypts are open to the public. I was surprised when one of the guardians motioned for me to go down the stairs leading to one. I glanced at our guide for a signal, and he motioned that it was all right to do so.

When I descended the stairs leading into the crypt, I had the strangest feeling. It was a small underground hallway and chamber where only a few people could walk through at a time. For some reason, I felt the same sacred sensation as when I had entered the Great Pyramid.

The guardian motioned for me to look at a wall relief of Horus and Hathor. He could not speak English, but he was using hand signals to tell me that to touch these images would bring healing. I followed his signals and found myself touching the wall with one hand and my abdomen with the other hand. Suddenly, there was instant relief from the abdominal pain that had developed during the trip. I marveled at this man, who seemed to know intuitively what I needed. It reminded me of what was taught about the ancient Egyptians: they possessed a type of intelligence referred to as "intelligence of the heart," an esoteric state of being considered the "Sacred Science" of their tradition. Needless to say, to me this crypt meant a healing chamber.

The statue of the "ka," the soul essence of Hathor, was kept in the crypts. This statue played a major role in the festival of the New Year. The ritual procession started while it was still dark in the early morning. The priest brought the statue of Hathor from the crypt through the sanctuary. Statues of other gods joined the procession in the Hall of Appearances, eventually winding their way up the western staircase. The king led the procession, with the priest behind him, wearing the masks of various gods. Then they entered the roof chapels, while chanting a hymn to move on to the head of the stairs to greet the dawn.

As the rays of dawn began to glimmer over the horizon, the statue of Hathor was disrobed and symbolically united with the sun disk. With this, the New Year began at the first dawn of light when "the goddess Hathor was united with the beams of her father, Re." This was how the text read on a nearby wall. And at this point the great festival began.

The Roof Chapels

The roof chapels to the North are devoted to aspects of the Osiris-Isis-Horus myth. In one chapel, Isis and Nephthys mourn the slain Osiris. In the next chapel gods are armed with knives to guard the gates to the Duat. Four chapels have to do with the resurrection of Osiris. But the most impressive is the Chamber of the Great Zodiac where the ceiling is carved with the famous circular Dendera Zodiac.

Cancer the Crab is shown in the center of the circle. The Hippopotamus represents Draco the Dragon. The hind leg of the ox represents the Great Bear, and Anubis is the Little Bear. Behind the Crab is Leo the Lion, and the rest of the signs are depicted counter-clock-wise. It has been determined by Egyptologists that the Dendera Zodiac was designed to prove that its symbolism purposely masked chronological information relevant to the origins of the Dendera temple. This has to do with the conflict of the sign of Cancer as the chronological birth of Egypt, as I mentioned before.

The Conflict

A conflict arose over the order of the zodiac at Dendera. Although all of the signs and symbols were represented, a prominent feature is given to Cancer, the Crab, as though this were leading the zodiac, followed by Leo and Virgo and so on, through the order of the zodiac. The question of this prominence of Cancer at the center of the zodiac arises again and again, because it leads the circular zodiac in the upper level on the roof chapel.

The same position of Cancer by the leg of the goddess Nut is also found on the ceilings of the tombs at Luxor. Nineteenth-century astronomers interpreted this placement of Cancer as a sign that the civilization of Egyptians began under the sign of Cancer.

At the time of the height of the Ptolemaic Dendera, the precession of the equinoxes was in the last degree of Aries. However, with the historical reading of Cancer as the rising sign of the equinox in the Nineteenth Century, this would have placed the age of Cancer between 8,000 B.C. and 6,000 B.C., creating a conflict in history.

In the Nineteenth Century, there was no archeology or chronology for Egypt. The Christian church was described as "fundamentalist" and convinced that the world was created by God in 4004 B.C. Dr. James Ussher, Anglican Archbishop of Armagh, Ireland, calculated the creation of the world to have been at October 22, 4004 B.C.

The historical evidence provided by Dendera created quite a stir to dispute that theory, and this dilemma continues until today.

I found it interesting that Cleopatra had been initiated into the royal threshold of "Pharaoh" during the annual festival of Dendera, because of the mystical importance of this great event. In fact, Dendera was a major Initiation Temple. Can't you just imagine Elizabeth Taylor as Cleopatra, carrying out this grandiose ritual before opening the momentous festival? (Elizabeth Taylor played a stunning role in the movie, *Cleopatra*.) Each year during the Ptolemaic rule, there was an enormous pilgrimage between the temples of Edfu and Dendera to symbolize the celebration of Horus and Hathor. The pilgrimage ended with wine and merrymaking, after a period of fasting.

The exterior facade of Dendera is covered with large reliefs and complicated texts. On the southern wall, huge reliefs symbolize a royal offering to the gods of Dendera. In the center of the rear wall, Hathor is shown communicating with the gods in the sanctuary, the Holy of Holies. The stone of this relic has been chipped away by pilgrims, a practice that has continued over the years. The defacements are a sign of the importance of such statues or reliefs.

The rear facade depicts offerings that were received by Hathor of Dendera, Horus of Edfu, and their son, and by Osiris, Isis and their son. Shown officiating at this ceremony are Cleopatra and Cesarion, her son by Julius Caesar, named Ptolemy XVI.

On the upper level of the roof of the Temple of Hathor, one can see the site of the former Sacred Lake used for rituals, now a huge cavity filled with vegetation. One can also get a beautiful view of the Nile Valley.

It is now time for us to leave this ancient, wondrous village of Dendera, a favorite place in the Land of the Gods.

CONCLUSION

The Garden of Eden was a symbol for a moment in time when there was an innocence of opposites, a knowing of unity, out of which developed a consciousness that later became aware of change, and the polarities, such as male/female, good/evil, active/ passive, hot/cold, etc., and the need to make a choice of which polarity we would choose to follow. The choice that is made determines whether the outcome is positive or negative.

During an interview with Bill Moyers, the respected television journalist for CBS News and PBS, Joseph Campbell stated:

"People say that what we're all seeking is a meaning for life. I don't think that's what we're really seeking. I think that what we're seeking is an experience of being alive, so that our life experiences on the purely physical plane will have resonances within our own innermost being and reality, so that we actually feel the rapture of being alive..."

I understand now that the Egyptians felt the rapture of being alive. The Egyptians that I have met have a real zest for living. And here is something to ponder: Is it because of the legacies that the ancient Egyptians left? Is it connected to the legacy that the physical was connected to a star in the higher realms?

Joseph Campbell, who said to follow what brings you bliss, was one of the best storytellers of all time. After reading his stories of primal societies, the reader can be transported to the wide deserts under the open sky, domed by the goddess Nut, or to an oasis of trees and water. From these scenarios, one can begin to imagine how the voices of the gods spoke through the wind, and the spirit of God flowed throughout the Nile River, and the earth blossomed as a sacred place—the realm of myths and legends—the Land of the Gods.

The land of Egypt has its own stories, its own song, yet somehow it is part of the music of the spheres, the music that pervades the universe. Each planet, each country, each person has his/her own keynote of music, all of which contributes to the makeup of the universe.

Without a doubt, Egypt is the Mother of Civilization. Zahi Hawass, Ph.D., Director of Egypt's Supreme Council of Antiquities, recently claimed that only 30 percent of the Giza plateau has been explored. That means that 70 percent is left to discover. A whole wonderful world still remains to be uncovered, the ancient past of which we only have remnants. And they have only just begun to tap into the land of the gods which yet contains the mystery of the ages.

In a recent A.R.E. (Association for Research and Enlightenment) conference that I attended, John Van Auken was the featured speaker. He said that the ancient Egyptians were not primitive, by any means. If they could build such megalithic structures, that no one can figure out, where does that leave us? Could it be possible that the Egyptians of the very ancient past had more knowledge than we possess today? Isn't it possible that this knowledge got lost, and is waiting for us to rediscover it?

In my chapter on the Zodiac and Aries, I mentioned Sais, Egypt. This is a small village in the western part of the delta of the Nile River. Because of substantial water damage, the ruins in this area have not received much attention. The tomb of a sixth-century priest from Sais was discovered in Abusir. From an Old Kingdom inscription, it is possible to observe that Sais adhered to the Old Kingdom beliefs. This includes the use of Pyramid Texts, which gave reference to an ancient lost civilization. In addition, this harkens back to a Hermetic text of Egyptian origin, called "The Sacred Sermon," that tells us of men of wisdom, sages, who lived before the Great

Flood and whose civilization was destroyed. It says: "There shall be memorials mighty of their handiworks upon the earth, leaving dim trace behind when cycles are renewed…"

The Edfu Building Texts, recorded on the walls of the Temple of Edfu, describes ancient beings who were sources of knowledge called "Sages." The "Sages" and other divine/human beings were considered "Companions of Horus," who were dedicated to bringing the knowledge of resurrection to humanity, much like the Brotherhood of Light. They were members of a brotherhood who came to earth to build temples according to a specific plan.

A Strange Discovery

How can we explain the symbols displayed in the Temple of Osiris at Abydos which show definite drawings of an airplane, helicopter and flying saucer? Abydos, located north of Karnak, is by far another most interesting site in Egypt. The Temple of Osiris is the temple of Pharaoh Seti, the father of Ramses II. It furnishes a list of the names of kings of ancient Egypt from Medes to Seti. Seti I was the pharaoh who originally began to build the temple which represents 2,000 years of history. Ramses finished the temple of his father at the time of Moses. In a 1999 article from *Enterprise Mission* by Richard Hoagland, he considered whether the drawings of an air transport could be a possible helicopter of the pharaohs. Just to make it more interesting, Edgar Cayce Reading 953-24 contains a question asking: "What was the mode of transportation during this period in Egypt?" The answer was: "In this period there was the caravan, a portion of the lost forces as were seen in the lighter than air, and the forces of the force, as given, propelling in water." How fascinating to think that air travel was possible in Egypt and Atlantis as recorded in the Cayce readings!

Another Strange Discovery

In 1898 in the tomb of Pa-di-Imen located in Saqqara, Egypt, a model airplane was discovered, dated at approximately 200 B.C. Largely because the birth of modern aviation had not even taken place, the strange wooden object was considered insignificant and sent to the Cairo Museum to be cataloged as Special Register Number 6347. It was not until 1969 that it was rediscovered by Dr. Khalil Messiha, an Egyptologist, who happened to be cleaning out the museum storage area in the basement when he came upon a box marked "bird object," within which he found the model glider. The contents within this box were small bird objects, but this object had modern aircraft designs. Since Dr. Messiha had been a model plane enthusiast, he recognized the amazing airplane features, and persuaded officials to form a committee in order to investigate this new find. The small model is made of sycamore wood, with an eye painted on its nose, and two redlines under the wings. The model's wings are straight and aerodynamically shaped. The total weight is only 39.12 grams. A separate piece fits into the tail, similar to the back tail wing of a modern airplane. It was decided that this was no toy model because of its scientific design. Aerodynamic experts said that the negative dihedral angle of the wing achieves the requirements for great lift force. The wing's surface provides stability in flight, while the aerofoil shape of the body lessens the drag. Although it was over 2,000 years old, the model plane can soar a considerable distance with a slight movement of the hand. The aerodynamic experts testified that the model was curiously airworthy, demonstrating acute knowledge of principles of aircraft design which had taken American designers a century of airfoil experiments to uncover. Even more surprising were the similarities between the model and the latest NASA findings in oblique-winged aircraft.

The hieroglyphs on the Egyptian model airplane said, "The gift of Amon," and Amon was described as the god of wind and air. In order for anyone to make a model airplane, there had to be an airplane for them to model it from. All of the books on Atlantis told of airplane travel. Could this have been also a part of ancient Egypt to where some of the surviving Atlanteans fled?

The Myth of Osiris and Isis

The story of Osiris and Isis is repeated in the lives of Jesus the Christ, Brahma and other icons of spirituality. This ancient legend follows a pattern of birth, life, death and rebirth. An individual born of a Virgin birth becomes a great spiritual leader. There is an eternal battle of

Good against Evil, and Evil has its way for some time before Good is triumphant. An individual dies and is reborn into another dimension or frequency (heaven).

The Egyptian gods seem to use magic for healings. Magic here means personal development by meditation and attainment at becoming one with the God light in the Great Central Sun. The lesson is to learn to use the power and energy that was given to us at birth, and to overcome negative emotions. Energy itself is neutral under the direction of the mind, which can be used for Good or Evil. Humanity lives under the Universal Law of Cause and Effect: Whatever is done to another person must be done back to the one who caused the effect. It is like the saying: "What goes around, comes around."

In mythology there is an element of synchronicity between what happens in the sky and the outside world, and what happens inside the heart of humanity. This is an important basis upon which lies the foundation of astrology as well. Perhaps this is why astrology has existed for so many years. The sun's drama of death and rebirth reflects the same process eternally taking place within the individual.

The human spirit is like a caterpillar. Eventually, the caterpillar gets tired of crawling on the ground. In its development, it progresses to a cocoon. The wings get developed while in the dark, uncomfortable cocoon. Some things can only develop in the dark. But because the Creator has a destiny for the caterpillar, the wings develop so it can burst out of the cocoon as a magnificent butterfly to freedom. From this beautiful transformation--the breaking forth of light—a new life begins.

We have lost the knowledge which the ancients brought to our planet. Where is it? Is it still hidden in some dark, secret place? In Edgar Cayce reading #440-5, he refers to records that are in "sunken portions of Atlantis" indicating that this is "near what is known as Bimini...in the temple records that were in Egypt," and further that records were carried "to what is known as Yucatan in America." Even more curious are the following questions, how will we find these records, or who will find them?

In Edgar Cayce reading #3976-15, he was asked, "Who will uncover the history of the part in record form which are said to be near the sphinx in Egypt?" He answered, "As was set in those records of the law of One in Atlantis, that there would come three that would make of the perfect way of life. And as there is found those that have made, in their experience from their sojourn in the earth, a balance in their spiritual, their mental, their material experiences or existences, so may they become those channels through which there may be proclaimed to a seeking, a waiting, a desirous body, those things that proclaim how there has been preserved in the earth (that as is a shadow of the mental and the spiritual reservation of God to His children) those truths that have been so long proclaimed. Those, then, that make themselves that channel."

According to Cayce, the three that would come, were individuals who had former lifetimes with the names of Hept-Supt, Atlan, and El-Ka. It would be necessary for them to be purified physically, mentally and spiritually, to enter the sealed room of the Hall of Records. Did Cayce mean purity of intention, selflessness or diet?

In Edgar Cayce reading #264-50 we get a glimpse of how the ancient Egyptians purified themselves through tests and initiations in the Temple of Sacrifice and the Temple Beautiful:

"9. First in the Temple of Sacrifice it became necessary, as indicated, for the signifying of the individual's desire, by its activity of purifying self through those days of purification - that later became exemplified in many of the forms of religious ceremony of purifying and preparation that there might be put away from the body and from the mind those things that would lead or direct or tend to make for the associations with the old self.

10. Then came the periods of passing through the testings that were set as near as possible to the fires of nature, that there might be the emptying as through those experiences that had made for those very influences that brought about the lower forces in the experience of the body.

11. So with this body, passing through those periods; and then the anointing with oil, the

passing through or raising of the vibratory forces within self, the activities and assistance through the priest and the activities that made for the burning of same as it were upon the altars of nature."

I would like to point out one aspect of the readings that begs to be understood. And that is the mastering of the science of vibration. The rate of vibration determines where the soul resides on the inner planes. The inner planes are the spiritual planes. Similar to the way a physical body earns the right to a decent place to live on the earth plane, so the soul earns the plane he/she occupies on the spiritual plane. Remember that the physical is connected to a star, the spirit, a higher plane in the universe. At whatever rate you are vibrating, you will be brought into the experiences that you find. Like attracts like, and that is a law of life.

After visiting Egypt, I began to understand how the voices of the gods spoke through the elements of air, water, earth and fire.

The essence of the sacred still remains in the ancient temples. The fire essence of Serapis Bey can be felt at the Temple of Luxor. It is felt through the uplifting vibration of the ascension flame which lingers on for those who can attune to it.

At the complex of Karnak, the healing vibration of Tefnut can be felt within the Holy of the Holies sanctuary. And at the Temple of Hathor in Dendera, healing can be experienced by touching the earthen stones in the underground crypts.

As you sail along the Nile waters in a felucca (a river boat), the peace of the Nile can be such a sensuous experience. You may be reminded of wistful days gone by, as you view men guiding their cattle, and women balancing water jugs on their heads.

Finally, in the Great Pyramid of Giza, the air has a different energy, that stimulates all five senses and well as the third eye, or brow chakra, where something higher than an earthly feeling exists. For each one who enters, the pyramid has an initiation that is just right for that individual.

Osiris is waiting to connect you to Orion, the higher dimension, to help you catch that beam from the earth to your star. Anubis is also there to guide you with his keen sense.

Yes, the spirit of God flows through the ancient legends of the past, to impart knowledge that can enlighten and inspire, to bring the imagination back to a sacred place that leads to rebirth.

I found what I was looking for in the Egyptian Mysteries. I found something that resonated deep within me. Perhaps it was a past life experience, brought alive by the contact with Egyptian places and stories. Perhaps it began with the first Egyptian I met with the light of recognition in his eyes, even though we had never met before in this lifetime. But one thing is certain: I found a rapture of being alive. And it came after I had experienced one of those lows in life when my soul was being tested. That's how it happens. The soul goes through the dark night before dawn in various stages of growth. As my grandmother used to say, "It is always darkest before the dawn." So look for your dawn when things seem the darkest. It will be there; it will follow.

I wrote this book out of love and rich experiences. May this reading experience resonate somewhere within your heart. May the knowledge contained herein touch you in some transcendent way. May something here connect with you, come alive within you, and bring you inner peace as well as joy.

LIST OF ILLUSTRATIONS

Illustration One: This is called the Oudjat, or Wadjet Eye (the Eye of Eternity) decoration on Egyptian coffins. Its purpose is to enable the departed to keep up with events in the world. This eye also had the power to conquer death, and represented the Eye of Horus. Belongings of the dead, such as furniture, clothing and jewelry were carried in boxes to the tomb to be buried with the corpse. It was common for the boxes to have images of the Oudjat Eye for protection, and Anubis, the guardian dog with the head of a jackal, to watch over them in the afterlife.

Illustration Two: Rah, the Sun God
Illustration Three: One version of Sekhmet
Illustration Four: Bastet, the cat aspect of Sekhmet
Illustration Five: The Benu Bird
Illustration Six: Hathor, as seen on the columns at the Temples of Dendera and Isis
Illustration Seven: Dogon Tribe Symbols
Illustration Eight: Khnum
Illustration Nine: Khnum creating the child prince on the potter's wheel
Illustration Ten: Neith
Illustration Eleven: Ptah
Illustration Twelve: Horus leading Hunefer to the weighing of the soul
Illustration Thirteen: Nephthys
Illustration Fourteen: Tefnut, an aspect of Sekhmet

Illustration Fifteen: Isis
Illustration Sixteen: Anubis
Illustration Seventeen: Set
Illustration Eighteen: Thoth, Am-mit and Sesheta
Illustration Nineteen: Hathor
Illustration Twenty: Amun-Rah
Illustration Twenty-one: Osiris with Isis and Nephthys
Illustration Twenty-two: Companion of Horus
Illustration Twenty-three: Bes

BIBLIOGRAPHY

This listing provides references to the material cited in this book, as well as additional material to supplement the reader's sources of information.

Aldred, Cyril, <u>Akhenaten, Pharaoh of Egypt: A New Study</u>, New York: McGraw-Hill Book Company, 1968.
Barker, Henry, <u>Egyptian Gods and Goddesses</u>, New York: Gross & Dunlap, 1999.
Barnes, Trevor, <u>The Kingfisher Book of Religions,</u> Hong Kong: Kingfisher Publications, 1999.
Bauval, Robert, Hancock, Graham, <u>The Message of the Sphinx</u>, New York: Crown Publishers, Inc., 1996.
Bonnefoy, Yves, <u>Mythologies, Volume One</u> Chicago: The University of Chicago Press, 1991.
Bowker, John, <u>World Religions</u>, New York: D. K. Publishing, 1997.
Budge, E.A. Wallis, <u>The Book of the Dead: The Papyrus of Ani</u>, New York: Dover Publications, Inc. 1895.
Bullfinch, Thomas, <u>Bulfinch's Mythology</u>, New York: Random House, Inc., 1993.
Campbell, Joseph, <u>The Power of Myth</u>, New York: Doubleday, 1988.
DeMailly Nesle, Solange, <u>Astrology: History, Symbols and Signs</u>, Hong Kong: Leon Amiel Publisher, 1981.
Dubos, Rene, <u>The Dreams of Reason</u>, New York: Columbia University Press, 1961.
Ebon, Martin, <u>Mysterious Pyramid Power,</u> New York: Signet, 1976.

Essene, Virginia, Kenyon, Tom, The Hathor Material, Santa Clara, CA: S.E.E. Publishing Co., 1996.

Fix, William, Pyramid Odyssey, Urbana, VA: Mercury Media, 1978.

Flanagan, G. Patrick, Pyramid Power, Marina Del Rey, CA: Devorss & Co., 1973.

Gabel, Creighton, Man Before History, Englewood Cliffs: Prentice-Hall, 1964.

Hall, Manly P., The Secret Teachings of All Ages, Los Angeles: Philosophical Research Society, Inc., 1977.

Hawkins, Gerald, Beyond Stonehenge, Toronto: Fitzhenry & Whiteside, Ltd., 1973.

Hathaway, Nancy, The Friendly Guide to Mythology New York: Penguin Putnam Inc., 2001.

Hurtak, J. J., The Book of Knowledge: The Keys of Enoch, Los Gatos, CA: The Academy For Future Science, 1977.

LePlongeon, Augustus, Maya/Altantis, Queen Moo and the Egyptian Sphinx, Blauvelt, N. Y., : Rudolf Steiner Publications, 1973.

Levi, The Aquarian Gospel of Jesus the Christ, Santa Monica, CA: Devorss & Co., 1972.

Luk, A. D. K., Law of Life, Book II, Oklahoma City: A. D. K. Luk Publications, 1960.

McDonald, Marianne, Mythology of the Zodiac, New York: Metro Books, imprint of Friedman/Fairfax Publishers, 2000.

McKenzie, Michael, Mythologies of the World, New York: Checkmark Books, 2001.

Morkot, Robert, Egypt: Gift of the Nile, Lincolnwood (Chicago): Passport Books, 1989.

Morley, Jacqueline, Egyptian Myths, Chicago: Peter Bedrick Books, 1999.

O'Brien, Joanne, Palmer, Martin, The State of Religion Atlas, New York: Simon & Shuster, 1993.

Parker, Julia and Derek, Parker's Astrology, New York: D. K. Publishing, 2001.

Read, Piers Paul, The Templars, New York: St. Martin's Press, 1999.

Renfrew, Colin, Before Civilization, New York: Alfred A. Knopf, 1973.

Robinson, James, The Nag Hammadi Library, San Francisco: Harper and Row, 1978.

Romer, John and Elizabeth, The Seven Wonders of the World, New York: Henry Holt and Company, 1995.

Schroeder, Werner. Man, His Origin, History and Destiny, Mount Shasta, CA: Ascended Master Teaching Foundation, 1984.

Sitchin, Zecharis, The 12th Planet, New York: Avon Books, 1976.

Tanner, Florence, The Mystery Teachings of World Religions, Wheaton: The Theosophical Publishing House, 1973.

Tomkins, Peter, Secrets of the Great Pyramid, New York: Harper & Row, 1971.

Van Auken, John, Ancient Egyptian Mysticism, Virginia Beach. VA: A.R.E. Press, 1999.

Verlag, H., The Power of Breath, Whittier, California: The Doty Trade Press, 1958.

Wilkinson, Philip, Illustrated Dictionary of Mythology, New York: D. K. Publishing, 1998.

Wilson, Colin, The Occult: A History, New York: Random House, 1971.

APPENDIX

ASTROLOCIAL SYMBOLS MENTIONED IN TEXT

SIGN		PLANETARY RULER OF SIGN	
♈	ARIES	♂	MARS
♉	TAURUS	♀	VENUS
♊	GEMINI	☿	MERCURY
♋	CANCER	☽	MOON
♌	LEO	☉	SUN
♍	VIRGO	☿	MERCURY
♎	LIBRA	♀	VENUS
♏	SCORPIO	♇	PLUTO
♐	SAGITTARIUS	♃	JUPITER
♑	CAPRICORN	♄	SATURN
♒	AQUARIUS	♅	URANUS
♓	PISCES	♆	NEPTUNE

CPSIA information can be obtained
at www.ICGtesting.com
Printed in the USA
BVHW021905250621
610516BV00017B/562